BATTLING
OCCULT
THE

Russ Parker

INTERVARSITY PRESS
DOWNERS GROVE, ILLINOIS 60515

Published in the United States of America by InterVarsity Press, Downers Grove, Illinois, with permission from Universities and Colleges Christian Fellowship, Leicester, England.

InterVarsity Press is the book-publishing division of InterVarsity Christian Fellowship, a student movement active on campus at hundreds of universities, colleges and schools of nursing in the United States of America, and a member movement of the International Fellowship of Evangelical Students. For information about local and regional activities, write Public Relations Dept., InterVarsity Christian Fellowship, 6400 Schroeder Rd., P.O. Box 7895, Madison, WI 53707-7895.

Distributed in Canada through InterVarsity Press, 860 Denison St., Unit 3, Markham, Ontario L3R 4H1, Canada.

All Scripture quotations, unless otherwise indicated, are from the Holy Bible, New International Version. Copyright © 1973, 1978, International Bible Society. Used by permission of Zondervan Bible Publishers.

Cover photograph: Michael Goss

ISBN 0-8308-1302-0

Printed in the United States of America ∞

Library of Congress Cataloging-in-Publication Data

Parker, Russ
   Battling the occult / Russ Parker.
     p.   cm.
   Includes bibliographical references.
   ISBN 0-8308-1302-0
   1. Occultism—Religious aspects—Christianity. 2. Occultism—
Controversial literature. 3. Demonology. I. Title.
BR115.03P37   1990
261.5'1—dc20   *90-38784*
                                                     CIP

13	12	11	10	9	8	7	6	5	4	3	2	1
99	98	97	96	95	94	93	92	91	90			

Acknowledgments

I would like to thank all those who have helped me and prayed for me as I prepared this book. Among the many I could mention, I would like particularly to say thank you to Michael Ross-Watson for his helpful comments and support; to Bob and Ann Ward for encouraging me to write in the first place; and to the home-group members in my parish who knew the issues at stake in the ministry of deliverance and who have given me their love and prayers. I would like to thank Yvonne, not only for typing the original manuscript, but for putting up with the endless changes I made and deciphering them all. Lastly and most importantly, I thank my wife, Carole, and my children, Emma and Joel, for understanding the pressures and problems of getting this particular book written.

1

The Occult Explosion

In April 1989 fifteen bodies were discovered in a mass grave in Matamoros, Mexico. Some of the bodies had been sacrificed in a type of black-magic ceremony by a "satanic, voodoo, drug-smuggling cult." As it turned out, the perpetrators were practitioners of a centuries-old folk religion called Palo Mayombe that had become syncretized with a nontraditional form of Satan worship. According to experts, there has been a significant rise in this self-styled Satan worship in the past years, especially among young people into heavy-metal music.

In a seemingly unrelated incident a fifteen-year-old boy in the United States shot himself to death after an argument with his father. His parents noted that his behavior before the suicide had become quite bizarre. During a simple game of backgammon, he had put a hex on his mother. In his case—and in at least fifty other instances of teen-age death, according to the National Coalition of TV Violence—the bizarre behavior can be linked to an obsession with the game Dungeons and Dragons. These two incidents highlight the revived and growing interest in the occult across the world today—and its far from innocent effects.

As Christians we have cause for concern. The occult does not only touch societal misfits; it's even being promoted in some public schools. Recently in England, a television company aired a series of programs related to occult interests. One participant, who writes horoscopes for a popular daily paper, said education authorities employed her to go into schools to instruct children in the use of horoscopes and tarot cards. Occult influences are becoming pervasive—and all too readily accepted.

Eminently Respectable
Recently a television company invited me to take part in a live, three-hour debate and discussion involving a number of practicing witches, a committed Satanist, a member of the nature cult of Isis, an acknowledged exorcist and a clinical psychologist. I was asked to represent the Christian point of view. The invitation came too late for me to accept, but I watched part of the program to see if anyone was there to uphold the name of Jesus Christ. As it turned out, Audrey Harper was present, a committed Christian who had formerly been a witch.

The thrust of the conversation was that Christianity was false and that Satanism and witchcraft were eminently fulfilling and respectable religions worthy of wider attention. The two witches were attractive young women, one of whom was a student archaeologist and the other the author of a considerable number of books (far from the haggard old women of the stereotype!).

It's no small wonder that the occult is gaining in popularity.[1]

Interest in the occult now generates business which can be measured in millions of dollars. Innumerable books on the subject range from how to develop your psychic powers to communicating with the dead. Just about every newspaper carries a horoscope column, and morning television includes astrology spots. Even the church seems to encourage this interest. It is not unusual to see a church social event advertising the presence of a fortuneteller.

The occult is gaining respectability. An article appeared a few years ago in the *Manchester Evening News* entitled "Witch Demands Apology." Mrs. Barbara Brandolani, a white witch, had complained to the Manchester branch of the National Council for Civil Liberties[2] (NCCL) concerning allegations made about her beliefs during a religious education lesson at school. A Christian guest speaker at the school her daughter attended had remarked that witchcraft was dangerous and anti-Christian. Mrs. Brandolani demanded an apology. The Manchester branch secretary for the NCCL stated that it was the society's policy that "witches should have the same rights to practice their religion as adherents of any other system of belief." Since witchcraft is anti-Christian, it is disconcerting that such a national organization should support it.

For some years now a week-long event, the Festival of Mind and Body, has been held in London. Many thousands have visited this exhibition, which deals with psychic phenomena, spiritual healing, palmistry, astrology, UFOs and forms of meditation. Numerous centers have sprung up around the country offering forms of alternative medicine such as hypnotherapy, yoga with relaxation routines and courses for developing psychic awareness. Also, a number of schools have begun to regard occult forces as examples of human potentiality and are offering classes in the scientific approach to the occult. Some modern cults, such as est and Scientology, equate the exercise of faith with drawing on these inner powers. Alongside the more "respectable" face of the occult is an increase in open involvement in magic and Satanism.

A newspaper recently carried an advertisement headed "Winning with Witchcraft" to promote a book with the same title. It stated:

> You can begin casting magic witchcraft spells to obtain whatever you desire . . . leave your physical body and travel anywhere [commonly called astral projection] . . . commanding things to happen through powerful spells and invocations.
> With witchcraft you don't have to grovel or pray to God.

However fanciful we might think these ideas are, at the heart of them is a clear rejection of trust and reliance on God.

There's Something There That Works

Interest in the occult has been furthered by a glut of films which focus on the power of evil, such as the *Omen* trilogy, *Friday the 13th* (and its seemingly endless sequels) and *Halloween.* Pioneers of this movie trend were *Rosemary's Baby* and *The Exorcist.* The last film, based on the book of the same title by William Peter Blatty, was about an incident which occurred in America in 1949. It featured a boy who was successfully delivered from evil spirits.

When *The Exorcist* ran in my area, local Christians gave out leaflets to the moviegoers outlining the dangers of occult involvement and including telephone numbers of Christian counselors they could contact should the film disturb them in any way. I was involved as a counselor and was quite amazed at the response. Among the dozen or so people who came to talk were committed Christians, people who had an interest in the occult but felt they had gone too far, and a small group of Mormon evangelists! They all felt that they had opened themselves up to something which disturbed them, and they wanted to be free of their fears.

The real danger with occult involvement does not necessarily lie in the activity itself (be it horoscopes, palmistry or even attending a spiritist meeting); it lies in the fact that by getting involved in such things we open ourselves up to that spirit of evil who masterminds spiritual deception at every level. As Paul wrote in his second letter to the Corinthian church: "The god of this age has blinded the minds of unbelievers, so that they cannot see the light of the gospel of the glory of Christ" (2 Cor 4:4).

Disobedience

Since becoming involved in deliverance ministry over twenty years ago, I have counseled and prayed with people involved in all aspects of the occult, from those who have dabbled in "harmless" activities such as reading horoscopes or playing with Ouija boards, to those who have been sexually abused in occult rituals. I have ministered to people dedicated to Satan at birth, people who have made blood pacts with Satan and those who became involved through parental or family influence or through involvements with cults or religious festivals. Their stories were different but the resulting bondage and oppression was the same.

These people often told me they got involved in the first place because they believed "there was something in this which seemed to work." I would go further and say that the "something" is in reality a "someone," namely, our spiritual enemy, the devil. He is described by Paul as "the spirit who is now at work in those who are disobedient" (Eph 2:2). Anyone, Christian or otherwise, who gets involved in the occult comes within the orbit of this spirit. Disobedience to God can ruin our Christian lives, and unless we respond with a truly repentant heart, we are heading for spiritual bondage.

Paul wrote some telling words about this in his letter to the church at Rome:

> Don't you know that when you offer yourselves to someone to obey him as slaves, you are slaves to the one whom you obey—whether you are slaves to sin, which leads to death, or to obedience, which leads to righteousness? (Rom 6:16)

Disobedience to God's rule, then, leads to slavery, and with it comes spiritual death. When that disobedience takes the form of involvement in the occult, we have clearly rebelled against God and turned to spirit resources which he has forbidden to us. We shall be defiled by occult contact (Lev 19:31). This defiling refers to the damage done to one's spiritual life when a person becomes affected by evil in the sight of God. Fellowship has been spoiled, and until the situation is cleansed, the individual is unclean and cannot come into God's presence.[3]

By giving ourselves to the sin of occultism we are liable to become its slaves and damage our spiritual well-being. We open up a door which may allow a spiritual enemy to gain access to our lives. Those who do this, soon find it hard to pray, and they cease to read the Bible; indeed they lose respect for it. Emotional stresses such as depression and anxiety may follow. They may desire to break free, yet they find themselves unwilling or unable to do so. This is spiritual bondage, and the only way to break free is to repent and turn back to God for forgiveness and cleansing. We shall examine the nature of spiritual bondage in more detail in chapter eight when we consider preparation for deliverance.

Deadly Games

A number of family or childrens' games have appeared on the market and have clear occult links. The most obvious of these is the Ouija board (the name combines the French and the German words for *yes*). It consists of a board with the letters of the alphabet around the edge. An upturned glass is placed in the middle of the board. Each player places the tip of a finger on top of the glass. In response to questions put to the spirit or the mind of the game, the tumbler is expected to spell out an answer. The game now outsells Monopoly as the number-one board game in America.

I have counseled a number of people, including children, who have been deeply disturbed at what happened when "playing" this seemingly innocent game. Answers have indeed come. In one case a local minister was called into a school where some pupils were in a hysterical and suicidal state, frightened by their experience of this game.

Along with books on magic and the supernatural, the Ouija board often leads the curious enquirer into an addiction to things magical and mysterious. They have led people into contact with forces outside of themselves, from which it is very difficult to get free. Psychiatrist Dr. Stuart Checkley says:

I have seen patients whose involvement with relatively minor forms of the occult has caused them to suffer mental illness. I have seen someone who as a result of one experiment with the Ouija board suffered frightening experiences outside his control, including automatic handwriting. He found himself writing frightening messages to himself.[4]

Some years ago the Christians of one town rallied together and lobbied the company producing this game so persistently that they ceased to manufacture it.

Another game, Osiris, was invented by an Australian clairvoyant who claims that it helps people develop their psychic ability. Alongside of this game are games such as Dungeons and Dragons, in which the use of magical forces is presented as good. The players are encouraged to imagine they are in a fantasy world, be it the Dark Ages or some futuristic setting inhabited by strange and powerful beings. These games usually center around combating the forces of evil and encourage teamwork to use magical powers to survive and possibly to win.

This kind of fantasy game can often open the door to the occult and glorification of evil. They can also incorporate gratuitous violence and horror. The following extract is from the "Dungeon Master's Guide" in Advanced Dungeons and Dragons:

> A wight is an undead spirit living in the body of a dead or demi-human. It can only be hit by silvered or magical weapons. Zombies are mindless undead humans or demi-humans animated by some evil magic user.

According to TSR Hobbies, manufacturer of the game, Dungeons and Dragons has sold over eight million copies since its creation in the early 1970s.

In the book *Children at Risk,* author David Porter goes into some detail about the wealth of magazines and material related to such fantasy games and points out that in this material children are being given virtually an encyclopedia of the occult and supernatural.[5] We put our children at great risk when we do this, and, sad to say, such items are easily purchased over the counter. Tragically, a number of small children become trapped in an obsessive interest in demons and evil. There is many a psychiatrist who will testify to having to work with disturbed children whose trouble began with a fascination aroused by such fantasy games. Magic is not good for anyone and does not improve the quality of life.

There are also a host of choose-your-own-ending books for children which invite the reader to exercise magical or occult powers. Reading these books surely courts danger. Early exposure to violence and occult or black-magic practices cannot fail to affect our values for the worse. Their perception of right and wrong can become confused. All too often, such confusion and disturbance are lived out later on.

Hard-Core Growth

Interest in the hard core of the occult, namely black magic and Satanism, is highly organized. An article in a local paper in 1986 reported that an organized alliance of Satanist groups had been operating in the area for about twenty years.[6] The article assured readers that those involved in these practices were not cranks but business executives, teachers and other professionals.

As a member of the Manchester Diocesan Deliverance Advisory Committee for a number of years, I can easily accept this statement. Between 1981 and 1985 our team was continually being called out to help people distressed through involvement with groups like this. On several occasions we had to care for people who were being physically attacked for daring to leave such groups. We estimated about a hundred such cases in the area we covered.

It is saddening to compare such a growth rate with trends in the church. In 1988 the Church of England had its lowest number of candidates for the ministry in this century (326). The Roman Catholic Church, similarly, has seen the number of men training for the priesthood in England drop continually, so that the number for 1988 was below 350. Yet in 1987 there were an estimated 52,000 spiritists in Britain. The spiritist churches report that their membership has doubled between 1982 and 1987. Compare this with the steady decline in numbers of those attending Britain's mainline denominations. The United States shows a similar increase in occult involvement. In 1971, 450 ministers of a particular Satanist church were ordained in one week, and the numbers of people involved in such groups have been rising since then.

I recently took part in a television program devoted to the subject of healing.[7] After the filming was completed, I talked to one of the reporters. He said that, based on the healings he had witnessed, he could see no difference between Christian and spiritist healing. Surely both were from God! After all, both used the laying on of hands and prayer.

His statement further drove home that we as Christians must wake up to the fact that (fakes and charlatans apart) there is a real power being exercised by spiritist healers, but it is not from the God of our Lord Jesus Christ; it is from an occult power or spirit. Nevertheless, their results captivate and deceive the public into thinking that spiritism must be good.

We Have an Enemy

Interest in the occult is sweeping the world. What is more, some of these occult groups are actively hostile to the Christian gospel and its practices. Not long ago, a number of Christian ministers were asked to support a fellow pastor who had recently taken a church openly opposed by a local coven. In one frightening episode, a relative of the new minister was waylaid on his way to the parsonage by a small group of people who said they had been waiting for him. He was to tell the new pastor to get out of their town, as Christian ministers were not welcome. No wonder the average length of time a minister had served there was two years! The minister certainly did need prayer.

Our spiritual enemy is real, and we need to understand the ways in which he gains access to peoples' lives so that when confronted by such problems we may deal effectively with them. Surely this is a necessary corollary to the prayer which Jesus taught us: "Deliver us from the evil one" (Mt 6:13). We shall lay the groundwork for this understanding in the next chapter.

2

Know Your
Enemy

The Christian church has always proclaimed the good news that Jesus saves. In order to do this, it has had to engage in spiritual warfare. The apostle Peter described this beautifully when he summarized Jesus' ministry: "God anointed Jesus of Nazareth with the Holy Spirit and power, and . . . he went around doing good and healing all who were under the power of the devil, because God was with him" (Acts 10:38).

This book does not aim to make an exhaustive study of the spiritual battles that face us but looks specifically at that area of evil which we call the occult. We have already seen some effects of occult involvement. We shall go on to explore the deliverance and healing which Jesus brings to those who want to turn away and be free from these effects.

The word *occult* comes from the Latin term *occultus,* which means "hidden, secret, sinister, dark or mysterious." The Christian life is just the opposite of that. We believe in a God who has revealed his love and his plan of salvation to humanity. Far from seeking to uncover what has been hidden from us, the Christian is to walk in the light of what has been shown to us. The journey into the occult begins with the curiosity of humans, but the journey with Christ begins with God coming to us through his Son with the offer of salvation. It is totally incongruous for Christians to be involved in the occult, for the occult neither comes from God nor helps us to grow in our faith through Jesus Christ.

The Devil: Always to Blame?

Before going any further, I must offer a few precautions and encouragements. First, let us not give our spiritual enemy, the devil, too much credit. A cartoon once pictured the devil crying outside a church. Someone asked him, "Why are you crying?"

He replied, "It's not fair! They blame me for everything in there!"

Not all our problems and difficulties are necessarily due to the presence of the evil one. Many are the consequences of choices we have made. If we have stored up bitterness or anger in our hearts, perhaps we don't need to be delivered, but to repent, to learn to forgive and to let God heal our lifestyle. Some people see the activity of evil spirits in every problem. They have a kind of "reds under the beds" mentality. This preoccupation with evil is unhealthy, to say the least.

One person who had been trying hard, but unsuccessfully, to give up smoking was told that his real problem was that he needed deliverance from a "spirit of smoking"! In *Pigs in the Parlour,* a practical guide to deliverance ministry, there is a list of fifty-two alleged demon groupings. Under these main headings are lesser demonic spirits such as daydreaming, headache, theatrics, driving, caffeine and legalism.[1]

We must be very careful when working with people who wish to see victory over some such habit. We may damage their sense of self-worth if we conclude that the problem is an evil spirit. What may be needed, rather, is repentance and self-discipline.

A Christian woman recently returned from a Christian conference claiming that her problems had been solved; she had been delivered from a spirit of depression and anger. But a couple of weeks later she felt angry and depressed again, despite maintaining a good spiritual life. Needless to say, she was very distressed. She thought that either the ministry had failed and she was still infected or that there were other spirits now surfacing for attention. I discovered that her husband was constantly overdrinking and that she was having to cope with problems with her children as well. I told her that she had a right to her anger and that it needed to be worked with rather than "cast out." With help, she was able to share with a group from her church how depressed she felt, and to let out the hurt feelings that were causing her depression. In doing this she found a great measure of release and is now working steadily for change in her home. It was not deliverance that she needed, but discussion and direction.

A Defeated Foe

It is good, secondly, to remind ourselves of the limitations of our spiritual opponent. The opening chapters of the book of Job clearly point out that the devil does not have anything like the power and insight of our great God and Savior. Satan, we are told, is answerable to God for his actions; twice he had to report to God his whereabouts (Job 1:7; 2:2). Satan's ability to attack a godly person is limited by the sovereignty of his Master (Job 1:12; 2:6). As Christians we need to grasp the utter superiority of God over evil.

It is not a case of two almost-equal forces, with the cause of good eventually succeeding. In the New Testament we are told that the devil is a defeated foe. As Jesus said when the seventy-two reported that even the demons were subject to them in his name: "I saw Satan fall like lightning from heaven. I have given you authority . . . to overcome all the power of the enemy" (Lk 10:18-19). Jesus clearly taught that through him we will overcome all evil. When confronted with evil, therefore, let us deal with it confidently through Christ. But we need to be careful about rushing into situations without due preparation, and we must also recognize that we may need experienced help. Chapter ten will offer some guidelines on a balanced procedure to help those in distress and in need of deliverance ministry.

The Devil's Tactics

Third, we need to be aware of the nature and tactics of our enemy. For one thing, he delights in rupturing Christian relationships. When Paul wrote his second letter to the Corinthian church, he was aware that there had been a breakdown in fellowship and that the church was hurting and in difficulties. He encouraged the Christians to forgive those who were sorry for their sins and to restore them to the fellowship. He went on to say that this was vitally necessary in order to keep Satan from gaining a foothold among them. He wrote: "We are not unaware of his schemes" (2 Cor 2:11). Paul knew the tactics of his spiritual foe! He was not going to let Satan destroy a church that was having difficulties restoring a fellow Christian.

Another of the enemy's tactics is to foster the belief that he and his demonic legions do not really exist! I once heard a wise Christian say, "The devil doesn't work overtime, he works all the time." This man was underlining the fact that we do have an enemy and we are engaged in spiritual warfare. Yet there are many Christians who dismiss the whole idea of evil spiritual powers as part of the cultural naiveté of the ancient Middle East.

Some have suggested, for example, that in their ignorance the early disciples understood certain strange behavior as being due to demon possession, though we now know that it was due to epilepsy. Jesus and his followers, they say, were limited to the world view of their day. Modern science shows that what was thought to be demonic is actually due to physical or mental illness. A closer examination of the facts, however, shows that this could not have been the case.

Look at this passage from the Gospel of Matthew: "People brought to [Jesus] all who were ill with various diseases, those suffering severe pain, the demon-possessed, those having seizures, and the paralyzed, and he healed them" (Mt 4:24).

These words show that Jesus and his disciples distinguished between physical illness and those sicknesses of the soul that were due to the activity of the evil one. Look at another passage, the one about the boy described as demon-possessed. His symptoms are listed as follows: "Whenever it seizes him, it throws him to the ground. He foams at the mouth, gnashes his teeth and becomes rigid. . . . It has often thrown him into fire or water to kill him" (Mk 9:18, 22). The boy's illness, though resembling epilepsy, was in fact caused by an evil spirit bent on destroying life.

Many doctors and psychiatrists are now coming to the conclusion that some of their patients need not the usual medication but deliverance from spiritual evil. Their conclusion is, paradoxically, more biblical than the opinions of some Christians on the cause of some bizarre behavior! One psychiatrist recorded this case history:

This 32-year-old, twice-married female was brought in because of falling spells which had been treated with all kinds of anti-convulsant medication. She was examined on the neurosurgical service and after all examinations including EEG, brain scan, and a pneumoencephalogram were negative, she was transferred to the psychiatric service. Her mental status examination was unremarkable and all of the staff commented that she seemed normal until she had her first "spell."

While standing at the door of the day room, she was violently thrown to the floor bruising her arm severely. She was picked up and carried to her room, all the while resisting violently. . . . Her facial expression was one of anger and hate. Sedation resulted in sleep. During the ensuing weeks, the patient was treated psychotherapeutically and it was learned that there was considerable turmoil in her childhood home, but because she was "pretty" she was spoiled. . . . After her second marriage she continued to associate with her "high living" friends. When her husband demanded she give up her friends and her parties, she started having the "spells." The usual psychotherapeutic treatment for hysteria including interviews under sodium amytol only aggravated her spells. Seclusion in the closed section brought her assaultive and combative behavior to an end, but she would have spells in which she became mute, especially when religious matters were discussed. More dramatically, when the names of Jesus or Christ were mentioned she would immediately go into a trance. On one occasion, while in a coma, in desperation, an exorcism was conducted and a demon was removed and her "spells" ceased. . . . The patient had recovered and been well ever since.[2]

This psychiatrist concludes his article by saying that, reluctant as he was to accept the activity of evil spirits, he nonetheless found that real healing came only when deliverance prayer in the name of Jesus was offered in faith. He said that a number of his patients had not responded at all to conventional treatment, and he was now convinced that what they really needed was spiritual help and deliverance from evil. I have myself worked in consultation with a number of family doctors and psychiatrists who have invited me to offer pastoral care and ministry to some of their patients, believing that the real need was to deal effectively with evil.

Unfortunately, many scientists have been reluctant to recognize the reality of evil. But, according to M. Scott Peck, this situation is rapidly changing:

We do not yet have a body of scientific knowledge about human evil deserving of being called a psychology. Why not? The concept of evil has been central to religious thought for millennia. Yet it is virtually absent from our science of psychology. . . . The major reason for this strange state of affairs is that the scientific and the religious models have hitherto been considered totally immiscible—like oil and water, mutually incompatible and rejecting. . . . For a whole variety of factors, the separation of religion and science no longer works. There are many compelling reasons today for their reintegration—one of them being the problem of evil itself— even to the point of the creation of a science that is no longer value-free. In the past decade this reintegration has already begun. It is, in fact, the most exciting event in the intellectual history of the late twentieth century.[3]

The Bible teaches that there is an evil spiritual power, called the devil. If people are to be set free to know their God, some degree of deliverance from evil will be involved. The glorious reality is that people can be completely set free from evil through the power of Jesus Christ. The man called Legion, from whom Jesus expelled many demons, sat "at Jesus' feet, dressed and in his right mind" (Lk 8:35). Let his testimony encourage us as we go on to examine how people become caught in Satan's web, and how they can be released.

3

Occult Doors I: Superstition and Fortunetelling

There seem to be four doors through which people go in search of occult fulfillment: superstition, fortunetelling, magic and spiritism. It is my experience that all four produce some degree of spiritual contamination. The next chapter will discuss magic and spiritism, but first we shall look behind the doors of superstition and fortunetelling to see what is there and where they lead.

Superstition

Superstition is one of humankind's oldest religious preoccupations. It has been described as "a form of personal magic used for coming to terms with the unknown." It is basically a lack of trust in God. The phrase *knock on wood,* for instance, according to some is a reference to a pagan ritual associated with the oak tree, or perhaps is a nominally "Christian" action connected with the cross that began first as a pagan ritual.

Some superstitions have, or have had, some basis in fact. The reluctance to be a third person to light a cigarette from the same match may be traced to the World War 1 trenches, when the enemy would have had time to load and aim at his victim during the first two lightings. Most superstitions, however, cannot be so definitely traced. But even Christians have been known to "knock on wood" or carry a rabbit's foot.

A Feeling of Security

Many superstitious remedies and activities are supposed to keep us safe. Sometimes they speak of dangers to be avoided, such as walking under a ladder or incurring seven years' bad luck by breaking a mirror. The origins of many such superstitions are now lost to us, but they still have power over many people. There are a host of remedies to ward off evil or gain good luck, such as throwing salt over your left shoulder. Though there is no rational reason for such practices, people do them to insure their safety or clinch their success.

It's customary for ships to be launched with the blessing "May God bless her and all who sail in her," and a bottle of champagne broken over her bow. Not many people question the ceremony, and yet no ship is considered to be seaworthy until the bottle is broken. Yet originally the act was performed to placate the gods!

Here is a classic example of the hold of superstition over peoples' minds. The original reason behind the practice may be long forgotten, but the practice itself is maintained because it makes us feel secure.

Some years ago a Christian wrote a book pointing out that

every American president elected to office at any of the twenty-year intervals after 1840 died in office (the presidents were Lincoln, Garfield, McKinley, Harding, Roosevelt and Kennedy). The rest of the book was devoted to the future in store for the then-new President Reagan. The writer felt that Reagan too would die in office because of the twenty-year cycle. This is nothing less than superstition dressed up with Christian trimmings. The twenty-year figure soon began to assume a life of its own in the mind of the writer. But surely as Christians we believe that our "times" are in the hands of God. For us, there is only one response to such fear and uncertainty about the future, and that is to base our lives on the solid reality of Jesus Christ as Lord and Savior.

John Richards underlines the modern technologist's fascination with superstition. There was great consternation when Apollo 13, launched at 1313 hours, met with near disaster on the thirteenth day of its mission. Ordinary launchings were enough to produce an army of crossed fingers; one of the flight directors insisted on wearing first a white, then a red and finally a gold shirt at specific stages of the mission.[1] Hotels and highrises, because of the same superstition, lack a thirteenth floor, and streets a house numbered thirteen. Some pilots would not consider taking off without first spitting on the steering column or installing a lucky charm.

The sports world abounds with superstitions. Before the start of each home game, the members of my favorite soccer team always give a good-luck pat to the club shield on the wall above the exit tunnel from their locker room—a ritual they say they'd never consider giving up. Somehow they believe their ability to win is bound up with this simple ritual. Other sports people have other superstitions which are supposed to help them win or keep them from harm.

By following superstitious customs, we put our trust in the unknown and the unsafe rather than in the God who has revealed his love for us in his Son Jesus Christ.

Lucky Charms

Millions of people would not dream of going out of the house without a charm of some description, be it a bracelet, key ring, coin, lock of hair or religious item blessed in church. Even crucifixes and St. Christopher medals assume the function of charms and are thought to bring good luck to the wearer. Over ten million rabbits' feet are sold in the United States every year. The sale of charms is a multimillion-dollar business. What the primitive Indian in the Amazon jungle wears for protection, his cousin in the city wears as a charm on his key ring.

A charm was originally a chant or incantation recited in order to produce some good or bad effect. (The term *charm* comes from the Latin for *song*.) An object may be charmed in this manner and then worn or carried. It is clear from Scripture that the charmer is condemned along with other occult practitioners. When Isaiah the prophet was pronouncing God's judgment upon Egypt, he painted a picture of cities in disarray and the nation as spiritually bankrupt: "And the spirit of Egypt shall fail in the midst thereof; and I will destroy the counsel thereof: and they shall seek to the idols, and to the charmers, and to them that have familiar spirits, and to the wizards" (Is 19:3 KJV).

Sources of Bondage

No matter how innocent and harmless the charms and amulets may appear, they are the thin end of the occult wedge. As such they endanger our spiritual health, and we must therefore rid ourselves of such things. Kurt Koch lists a number of case histories where individuals needed help and deliverance from spiritual oppression. The root of their problems was that they had been in the habit of wearing a charm, a locket, or a bracelet which had been subjected to a spell of some kind.[2]

Some years ago, I counseled a young man who was slowly emerging from a homosexual affair and who was seeking to get his life back in order with Jesus Christ. Something still seemed to be holding him back. During a time of prayer he happened to mention the ring he was wearing which his former partner had given to him as a mark of their relationship. It turned out that this ring had been charmed by a medium. The ring was immediately removed and given up. He repented again of his former lifestyle and renounced the ring and all it stood for. From that time on, he noticed an immediate release and knew he was free from what had held back his spiritual growth. He had new resources to take up the cross and get on with his life as a Christian.

Halloween

Another popular superstition is Halloween. Most children can tell you about it. They know it has something to do with witches because many schools get their children to make witch costumes and jack-o'-lanterns. Then there are the associated games, such as dunking for apples, and trick-or-treating throughout the neighborhood.

In the church's calendar, Halloween—or All Hallows Eve— is the night before All Saints' Day, which celebrates the Church Triumphant; it was seen as the night when the spirits have their fling before they are declared defeated. What really lies at the heart of Halloween, however, is a desire to placate the forces of evil. It is a christianized version of the ancient Celtic ritual of Samhain, which was held on October thirty-first. It marked the end of the summer and so formed the Celtic New Year's Eve. Bonfires were lit to frighten away evil spirits. Samhain did not attempt to get in touch with evil forces but was considered a necessary ritual to ward off any harm that may come. It was also seen as a good time for divination about death, health, marriage and luck. It is not surprising, then, that it lent itself to the practice of other occult activities.

The modern Halloween has made respectable the interest and pursuit of the occult. In 1965 UNICEF introduced collections at Halloween for the United Nations Children's Fund. In 1986 the Girl Guides magazine *Guider* produced an article on how to hold a safe and enjoyable Halloween party. In response to a letter I wrote criticizing the article, I was told that such activities are harmless and do not oppose the Christian faith. But I fail to see how popularizing evil can be described as harmless.

Not even churches are immune from this practice. After a television interview on Halloween, in which I took part, the sound man turned to me and said that he could see no harm in it. After all, the nuns at his daughter's school were helping to make the witches' costumes and masks!

Lovable Little Witches

When I began my ministry in one church, I was disturbed to find the church's play-school children decorating the church room with silhouette cutouts of witches. When I asked why the children were doing this, the leaders replied that it was only harmless fun and that Christians must not be seen as killjoys. "We mustn't spoil the children's fun as it would put them off coming to church."

I explained to the play-group leaders that Halloween makes evil appear fun. To their credit, they removed the paper witches from the church walls and instead played harmless games not associated with jack-o'-lanterns or trick-or-treat. There were no complaints from the children!

In the opinion of Dr. David Enoch, former senior consultant psychiatrist at the Royal Liverpool Hospital and the University of Liverpool, Halloween practices open the door to the occult and can introduce forces into people's lives that they do not understand and often cannot combat.

Much damage is done by Christians who mix up Christianity with the occult by encouraging this practice, which is pagan at heart. For too many children, this annual preoccupation with evil leads to a deepening fascination with the supernatural, witches and the possibility of exercising power over others.

In the United Kingdom, the Association of Christian Teachers has produced a leaflet entitled *Hallowe'en*[3] in response to this popularization of something intrinsically evil. They underline three reasons for concern about Halloween as an educational exercise.

1. If we suppose that witches and spirits are nonsense, why, then, encourage children to celebrate their mythical frolics and perhaps take them seriously? Paganism is hardly a cultural mainstay of all that is best in our society.

2. Suppose that in our folklore, witches and demons merely represent moral evil. Hallowe'en then tends to celebrate evil in the ascendant by the reversal of moral standards. If Nazi figures were regularly presented for children's admiration and affection there would soon be a public outcry. But lovable little witches are brought out every autumn. This disturbs the polarization of good and bad, right and wrong, in children's minds.

3. Hallowe'en does in fact encourage an interest and fascination in the occult and this invariably leads to more serious involvement and damage to the individuals concerned.

Harmless Nonsense?

The true importance of superstition lies in the fact that it usually leads to deeper involvement in the occult. John Richards points out that the superstitious do not understand their position and are thus exposed and insecure.[4] At the heart of the superstitious practice is an admission that the individual feels vulnerable to the forces that exist in the world. Though superstitious persons may claim to be Christians, they demonstrate that they are not: instead of depending on God for their salvation, they rely on their charms or superstitious actions. For the committed Christian, superstition verges on the blasphemous, for it gives to created things, such as black cats, mirrors, salt and wood, those powers which belong only to the Creator.

It is not enough for people to say, "It's just a bit of harmless nonsense." If it is, why not give it up and trust in God alone? When I have challenged superstitious people in this way, I have found that they suddenly cling hard to their beliefs and will not let them go. Superstition is thus shown for what it is, an act of defiance against the clear command of God. Paul's words aptly sum up the superstitious mind: "They exchanged the truth of God for a lie, and worshiped and served created things rather than the Creator" (Rom 1:25). Superstition is symptomatic of people who know they are insecure but who will not put their trust in their God and Savior.

Fortunetelling

Fortunetelling is the second occult door behind which we are going to look in this chapter. The practice takes many forms. It underlines the basic need of all people for purpose and a path in life. The quest for knowledge of what is to come is really an attempt to take control of our own future without trusting in God to take care of us.

The most common form of fortunetelling is the horoscope. According to one opinion poll, twice as many people read their horoscopes every week as read anything from the Bible. Many read them "for fun." They may not realize that those who prepare the horoscopes for the popular papers are usually committed astrologers who take their craft very seriously. For example, television astrologer Russell Grant is a founding member of the British Astrological and Psychic Society. On his nationwide zodiac telephone hotline he recently advised so-called Capricorns, "If you've always wanted to study psychology, the occult or the paranormal, then now's the time to begin."

Despite his friendly and jovial approach, Russell Grant is a committed occultist. And occult practices open doors to spiritual forces which can wreck lives.

The basis of astrology is the alleged influence of the planets on peoples' lives—past, present and future. This belief is prohibited in the Bible. The tower of Babel (Gen 11:1-4), for example, was not the world's first attempt to build a skyscraper. Quite possibly it was a ziggurat, or tower, with the signs of the zodiac (a chart of the heavens) at the top. These were typical of the religion and culture of Babylon and Northwest India two thousand years before Christ. They served as astrological observatories, with temples at the top for star worship.[5] If the tower of Babel was indeed a ziggurat, astrology probably ranks as the first religion to present itself as an alternative to trust in the one true God.

A lot of people take astrology very seriously indeed. It is well known that some businesses employ a professional astrologer before embarking on any major ventures. Many newspapers advertise the services of professional astrologers who for a fee will prepare complete character analyses of their clients. The noted psychiatrist Carl Jung used astrology to form character assessments as guides to therapy for his patients.

Astrological Predictions
In 1988 Donald Regan, chief of staff at the White House during the Reagan administration, published a book entitled *For the Record*. In it he devoted considerable space to the fact that the president's wife, Nancy, consulted a professional astrologer, Joan Quigley, in order to plan her husband's schedule. Regan maintained that her predictions told the president when it was safe to fly and when it was not. The astrologer, who confirmed the reports on national television, added that the president should not have gone to the Reykjavik summit meeting with Mr. Gorbachev of the Soviet Union because the time was not favorable.[6]

The extent to which such interests preoccupy and ensnare people's minds with fear was graphically demonstrated in Los Angeles during May 1988. There was widespread panic selling of property in the city because a film had been released which told the story of the sixteenth-century astrologer Nostradamus and his prediction that there was to be a severe earthquake in Los Angeles on May eleventh of that year. A local real-estate agent began reporting an extraordinary rise in the sale of property as people endeavored to sell and move out. A local astrologer gave relaxation responses over the telephone to the many who called in because they were anxious.

The panic became so acute that the Griffith Park Observatory recorded a message on its answering machine telling callers that there was nothing to fear.

There are two kinds of astrologers, the mathematical and the mantic. The former base their predictions on mathematical evidence and statistics, focusing on personal traits and individual character. The second type employ a divinatory approach. This, at its most basic, involves subjectively reaching into the client's emotional state, coupled with suggestions which build on this knowledge. At the more sophisticated end of the scale is the operation of a definite spirit power which is very obviously not the Holy Spirit.

The well-known fortuneteller, Jeane Dixon, attends the Catholic Mass and prays the twenty-third psalm, and many consider her powers and experiences to be from God. Yet when questioned about a New Testament account of the destruction of occult literature (Acts 19:18-20) by former occultists who had now put their trust in God alone for the future, she replied that this belief was no longer relevant for Christians.

Cards and Crystals

Other forms of fortunetelling include palmistry, crystal-gazing, card-reading, automatic writing and the Ouija board. They all involve a deliberate surrendering to outside forces, be they psychic or spiritual. Crystal-gazing, for example, is not the ability to see events in the crystal ball itself. This may be the impression given by practitioners at tourist traps or carnivals, but serious-minded gazers use the ball only as a means to focus on or to tap into their powers of clairvoyance. These practices include interpretation and guidance, and they exert great influence over their clients. They rob them of their ability, under God, to determine their future and to make choices for themselves. To submit to the appeal of fortunetelling is to take a very dangerous step into the realm of occult forces, which can only harm us.

> A young woman whose husband was missing from the Eastern front went to a card reader to find out whether he was alive. . . . The fortune teller replied, "Your husband is dead." The wife waited three months, and again visited a card reader to find out about the uncertain fate of her husband. Again the answer was, "Your husband will not return." She went home in despair, and turning on the gas killed herself and her two children. The next day the husband returned from a Russian prison camp, and found the dead bodies of his three loved ones.[7]

Possibly the card reader in question was just responding to the woman's own fears or had been deceived by the demonic forces behind such practices. Whatever the truth of the case, the effect of trusting in something outside of God is destructive. It fosters a dependence on the unknown and leaves the individual wide open to manipulation by forces which are anything but holy. The Manchester Deliverance Group continually encountered people suffering from depression and neuroses arising from an involvement with fortunetelling. Relief for them came only with repentance and prayer in the name of Jesus Christ.

Superstition and fortunetelling, then, are far from harmless. But if these things, often taken so lightly, are serious matters, how much more so are the more sinister phenomena of spiritism and magic! To these we must turn in our next chapter.

4

Occult Doors II: Spiritism and Magic

In the last chapter we explored what lay behind two of the main "doors" through which people are drawn into the world of the occult. Now we must look behind the doors labeled "spiritism" and "magic."

Spiritism

Some years ago, the well-known British actor Peter Cushing stated in an interview that he had found life very hard after the death of his wife, whom he loved very much. He went on to say that his grief led him into spiritism. At a séance his departed wife spoke some words of comfort to him through a medium. Since then he felt more able to get on with his life, for his wife was with him again, but from the spirit side.

Other notable personalities who have found comfort through spiritism are Sir Arthur Conan Doyle (the inventor of Sherlock

Holmes), William Gladstone and Bishop Pike. The last two were both directed to spiritism by grief at the death of their sons. These stories could be multiplied many times over. I once spoke to a group formed to offer companionship and help to the bereaved. Quite a few members told me that they had been approached by representatives from local spiritualist churches with alleged messages from their departed loved ones. Needless to say, some of them had subsequently become members of the spiritist movement.

Origins

Spiritism as an organized religion has its origins in 1848 in Hydesville, New York. Margaret and Kate Fox heard rappings in their home and, believing them to be sounds from the unseen spirit world, they devised methods of communication. The spirit was to reply to their questions according to a definite pattern. News of this phenomenon spread rapidly; soon séances and interest in spiritism became widespread in America, England and Europe. The Fox sisters who founded the movement, however, led tragic lives. In time, they became addicted to drink; nothing could satisfy their craving for alcohol, and they lost all sense of moral responsibility. Margaret, in the presence of her sister Kate, declared at an antispiritist meeting in 1888: "I am here tonight, as one of the founders of Spiritualism, to denounce it as absolute falsehood . . . the most wicked blasphemy the world has ever known."[1]

This was a bitter and ironic end for the sisters, especially as it is reported that the first message which they received was as follows: "Dear friends . . . you must proclaim these truths to the world. This is the dawning of a new era, and you must not try to conceal it any longer. When you do your duty, God will protect you and good spirits will watch over you."[2]

They certainly were not protected; their hoped-for blessings turned out to be curses indeed! But, despite what happened to them and others, the movement continued to spread.

Spiritism and Christianity

To be fully admitted into the National Spiritualist church one must agree with the following seven principles:

1. The fatherhood of God
2. The brotherhood of man
3. Communion of saints and the ministry of angels
4. Human survival after physical death
5. Personal responsibility to answer for one's own sins
6. Compensation or retribution for good and evil deeds
7. Eternal progress of every soul

At first glance, much of this may appear acceptable to the Christian. For the spiritist, however, the life and death of Christ give us only an example to follow; there is no saving quality to his death. Indeed, the president of the Union (allegedly the spirit of the late Conan Doyle) once stated regarding salvation from sins: "None can shuffle out of that atonement by an appeal to some vicarious sacrifice."[3]

Spiritism has grown and developed from people's need to find reassurance about their place in the universe. The letting go of loved ones to the world beyond is something too threatening for them, and so they find great comfort in maintaining a link with them after death. This prevents the proper processes of bereavement, whereby grieving people learn to accept their loss and to adjust to the future. Consequently, they store up their pain and do not allow themselves to give voice to their grief. Healing is still to come.

The contrast with Christian teaching could not be clearer. We are taught that when a Christian is "away from the body" he is "at home with the Lord" (2 Cor 5:8). Further, we have the promise of the resurrection to eternal life, and this has been guaranteed by the fact that Jesus has risen from the dead. When a death occurs in a Christian family, of course it is painful to let go. But we shall be together again at the Second Coming of Jesus Christ. And the Christian belongs to "the communion of saints," as the church's creeds describe it; those Christians who have died are still part of the body of Christ. They are like a great cloud of witnesses whose faith encourages us. The spiritist belief of communication from beyond is in direct contradiction to this biblical teaching.

Mediums and Sensitives

For those involved in spiritism, the link between the spirits and the seeker is the medium or "sensitive." In order to attract what mediums call benign spirits, meetings often commence with a prayer or with hymns specially written by their own members. The sensitive goes into a self-induced trance and then speaks or acts without the slightest knowledge of what is taking place. It is assumed that in this state the sensitive will speak with the voice of the departed person concerned.

Spiritists claim that departed spirits who have reached a higher spiritual plane can communicate teachings and knowledge to mankind, as well as heal the sick through the hands of the medium. Such spirits are designated as "guides." Some sensitives claim to be vehicles for the spirits of St. Paul, Francis of Assisi, Mozart or other people of great talent. If that were true, their messages should rate among the greatest and most inspiring ever given; yet this is far from the case. Most of the messages seem bland and trivial. Some directly contradict the Christian gospel, and this would be strange indeed if the saints were speaking.

The case of Bishop Pike is well documented; he asked his deceased son, through a sensitive, if he had heard anything about Jesus Christ. According to the bishop's own account, the answer he received was that no one knew anything personally about Jesus, as he was not talked about in that place.[4] This hardly agrees with the vision in the book of Revelation where the heavenly host continually fall down before the throne and worship the Lamb of God who is worthy of all praise and glory and majesty!

Spiritist Healing

Healing and psychic surgery are other aspects of spiritism. Many people claim to have been healed through the laying on of hands with prayer by a medium. These mediums may claim to have spirit guides with healing powers—some even claiming guidance from Lister or Pasteur. Spirit healers, unlike sensitives, do not go into a trance in order to do their work. The well-known British healer Doris Stokes would use large and well-lit auditoriums for her work, and there was thus no question of trickery and fraud. Some perform psychic "surgery": with the aid of spirit guides, diseased or damaged material is removed by hand from patients' bodies without the need of anesthetic or surgical instruments.

Whatever we may think of these practices, there is never a shortage of clients or claimants to healing. A number of Christian counselors experienced in this field have pointed out that people claiming to have experienced physical healing in this way have often developed emotional and spiritual anxieties. Doctor

Kurt Koch says that people healed through the influence of mediumistic forces suffer a deathlike blow to their faith.[5]

In my own counseling experience I have certainly found this to be true. I was asked to talk and pray with a young woman who was having nightmares involving considerable violence and bloodshed. Consequently she was feeling very disturbed and anxious. She came one day with her minister, who was present to offer support. She told me that she was a Christian who, despite a fairly difficult childhood, had grown up to be quite a stable person. She had been feeling depressed at one time, however, and had sought the help of a medium who prayed over her. Almost immediately the depression seemed to lift, and she felt much happier. This did not last for long, for the depressions returned, along with increasingly disturbed dreams. She also noticed that her Christian faith began to diminish and she found it very hard to pray or talk with her minister, something she had always managed to do earlier.

I pointed out to her that the Bible expressly forbade spiritism. She repented, and with further counsel the disturbing nightmares ceased. Once again her Christian life began to grow and develop. Incidentally, soon after our meeting her husband began to show a real interest in becoming a Christian and eventually came to a living faith in Jesus Christ.

Other Phenomena

Broader spiritist interests include clairvoyance and clairaudience (respectively, the ability to see and hear supernatural things), psychometry (the ability to make contact with absent persons, alive or dead, through handling their possessions), dowsing and water divination. There are also physical manifestations which allegedly allow onlookers to see, hear or feel the spirits for themselves. The spirits make use of a substance, supposedly drawn from the medium's own body, which takes the form of a departed person. The substance, called "ectoplasm," has been known to be handled when permission was given, although sudden contact has caused the medium great pain, resulting in physical harm.[6]

Such happenings have prompted a great deal of investigation by scientists as well as church people. There is a growing consensus that a real power is at work. The scientists in particular have used the term *psychic* to describe what they see as the human origin of such powers. This term encompasses the ability to read minds (extrasensory perception), to levitate or to move objects without physically touching them (telekinesis). Some mediums say that this is the power by which they are able to receive communication from the departed spirits or to project their astral bodies to another location. This psychic force is said to be spiritually neutral and inherent in all people; if everyone developed these God-given powers, their argument goes, we too could perform similar feats. In the next chapter we shall see whether this is true.

Magic

Our fourth door into the occult world is magic. At the heart of all magical endeavor is the desire to bring the spirit world under one's own control.

Magic normally falls into the two categories of black and white. Black magic seeks to control enemies while white magic seeks to benefit friends. White magicians claim that their power is from God, and they use Christian symbols such as the cross or the fish. The name of the Trinity is often used. Often there is the threefold repetition of the Lord's Prayer coupled with the use of three crosses, three Bible verses and three candles. (Carroll Thompson's *Possess the Land* says that white magic parallels Christianity in various respects. The occult invocation is the counterpart of prayer; the charms counterfeit Scripture; symbolic actions mimic the laying on of hands and baptism; and handling fetishes provides a physical contact for faith, as does the Lord's Supper in Christian worship.)

Both black and white magic seek power in order to control. This clearly contradicts the Christian gospel, which teaches that we are given power in order to serve others.

Satanism

Satanism typically follows from black magic and involves the worship of the devil as lord of the universe—in open opposition to Jesus Christ and his church. Besides offering worship to Satan, Satanists are encouraged to exercise mind control over others and have a belief in the power of curses. This power, though some may dismiss it as autosuggestion or a form of hypnosis, is well documented. Doctor Hugh Trowell gives the following account:

> I had a note from the Superintendent of Police saying that the man . . . had been bewitched . . . and was convinced that he would die that night at midnight, and would I examine him. I did so and found nothing wrong with him and sent him back to duty. . . . I saw him on my evening round, sitting on the bed dejectedly. . . . The Assistant told me that he watched him from the other end of the ward, that he never moved until the first stroke of twelve, when he had fallen back (dead) on his bed.[7]

These powers are real, and we need to remind ourselves as Christians that we have the protection of Christ whose peace

rules in our hearts. Of the many people I have talked to who
have decided to leave such Satanist groups, most have shown a
real fear of being harmed by the powers and influence of their
former associates. (It is well known, too, that these groups are
opposed to the Christian church and have broken into churches
where they have stolen communion wafers and performed certain rites.) But those wishing to break free have found release
through repentance and faith in Jesus and through prayer with
the laying on of hands for support.

Satanism is well organized and attracts many followers. Doreen Irvine, in her book *Spiritual Warfare,* describes the lavish-
ness of Satanic places of worship and the great care taken to
guard them.[8] In addition, most worshipers are not society's
dropouts but bankers and teachers, respected members of the
community.

Satanists must not be underestimated; putting aside those
groups which use this term merely as a cover for sexual and
psychic pastimes, there are those who are extremely serious
about their worship of Satan. Irvine mentions a girl who had
her hand severed in a worship service in order to prove her love
for Satan. No wonder Jesus said that "the thief comes only to
kill and destroy" (Jn 10:10). As Christians, we must take our
spiritual enemy very seriously and realize that one of Satan's
purposes is to destroy anyone he may devour. He hates human
beings and cannot abide to see the presence of God's new life
within them.

There are a number of reasons why people become involved
in something that is so openly anti-Christian. Sometimes it is
drug dependence that turns people in this direction; many drug
users report having religious experiences while taking drugs,
and these experiences can lead to Satanism. Others become in-

volved because of their attraction to free or perverted sex. This has led to blackmail, as some have been photographed unawares during these times. They are then under others' control and can be further manipulated.

Some are attracted to Satanism because they feel that the presence of Satan is much more immediate than that of God. Earlier I mentioned the comments of a television sound man in connection with Halloween. He went on to ask, "Why is it that the power of Satan is much more obvious than the power of God?" He pointed to the escalation of evil and the decline in church attendance. I responded by asking him to give me a few examples of the positive value of such experiences. Had they helped anyone to become more loving and patient? Did they help to bring families together in harmony? We concluded that the power of Satan was destructive and that Satanism could produce only gimmicks to attract the easily persuaded.

Witchcraft

There is a lot of confusion between witchcraft and Satanism. The term *witchcraft,* and the older word *wicca* from which it came, has been used by some to cover activities that include the worship of mythological nature gods. Others have used the term to describe magical practices. Still others understand it to refer to traditional wisdom concerning nature that gives a secret and spiritual interpretation to the world and the events around us. To make the confusion complete, some witches consider themselves to be Satanists as well.

This confusion was demonstrated on a recent British television show.[9] Part of the program was devoted to a confrontation between Jeffrey Dickens (a member of Parliament) and representatives of witchcraft in general. Dickens said that he wished to see witchcraft banned from this country, citing the child abuse he had discovered to be involved in witchcraft. He went on to say that as a Christian he felt it was wrong for witches to worship the devil, and he believed that they were leading their children into harmful practices. Those representing the witches said that they were horrified at such practices and that they in no way worshiped the devil or Satan. Indeed, one of them went on to say that Satanism was a Christian activity; the devil was after all an invention of Christianity! As much as I as a Christian would have nothing to do with witchcraft, I felt that their shock was genuine and that Dickens was perhaps speaking of Satanists or particular covens which include an element of Satanism. Whatever the truth may be, there is a great deal of confusion about what witches actually believe and practice.[10]

The image of a witch that immediately comes to mind is that of a hook-nosed old woman in a pointed hat. A very different picture is painted by Doreen Irvine in her autobiography, *From Witchcraft to Christ*.[11] Once "queen of the witches," she reveals that witchcraft, like Satanism, is busy attracting young people, as well as middle-class executives. It is also openly opposed to Christian values.

John Richards believes that the rise in witchcraft is related to the church's inability to convey the healing so greatly needed by people of our day, healing that witchcraft claims to offer. In a popular magazine of the late 1960s called *Man, Myth and Magic,* an article by a high priestess of witchcraft defended her craft, playing down the more obvious distinctions between it and the Christian gospel, while highlighting her craft's power to heal:

Witchcraft, despite its trappings, is just another way of life. The gods whom we worship symbolise the creative forces which made the universe and which our ancestors worshipped long ago. Our religion has the same purpose as other religions except that we believe that the creative forces can lend us power to heal and do good generally.[12]

While claiming to know God and offer fellowship in the name of Jesus Christ, the church has in reality all too often offered a dull and lifeless worship with little warmth or enthusiasm. Through continuous renewing by the Holy Spirit, however, the Christian church will be both dynamic and loving. It will then be able to offer fulfillment and purpose in life, which will bring healing to the seeking soul.

A Power That Is Real

When we have dismissed all that is fake and false, we are left with a power that is real. Does this power come from God? If not, where does it come from? Is there any scientific explanation of occult power, or is there a spiritual source which we need to discover? I believe that behind the occult phenomena is an evil power which is fundamentally anti-Christian and which originates with Satan.

Martyn Lloyd-Jones wrote these words:

The modern world, and especially the history of the present century, can only be understood in terms of the unusual activity of the devil and the "principalities and powers" of darkness. . . .

In a world of collapsing institutions, moral chaos, and increasing violence, never was it more important to trace the hand of the "prince of the power of the air." If we cannot discern the chief cause of our ills, how can we hope to cure them?[13]

In our next chapter we shall seek to trace that evil hand as it attracts people to the occult and deceitfully ensnares them in demonic captivity.

5

The Occult Attraction

We have looked at four ways in which people are led into the occult. Real forces are at work, and this fact reinforces many people in their desire to pursue their experiences to greater depths. In this chapter we explore some reasons why people become attracted to the occult.

Fear of the Future
Many people are apprehensive about the future, whether in this life or the next. The modern interest in spiritism in the West arose at the time of the great loss of life in the two world wars. Many grieving families found comfort in hearing that their deceased relatives were happy and living in peace on the other side.

Some people feel insecure and simply want to know what lies

just around the corner. This is surely the main reason why some read their horoscopes, even though they protest that it is just for fun. They need to be told that all will be well. Most occult predictions offer reassurance, telling inquirers that now is a good time to make decisions or to take a vacation or that good fortune is on the way. Sometimes predictions warn that it is *not* the right time to undertake a course of action. It all boils down to guidance on whether some activity is or is not safe at the moment. This underlines that many people live in fear and insecurity. Superstition and occult practices are attractive because they appear to meet a need for security regarding the future.

The Desire for Power
We have already seen that magic is a quest to have power over others. Christians have the promise of Jesus that we shall receive power when the Holy Spirit comes upon us. This power enables us to witness for Christ, follow his example and serve others.

The holder of occult power, by contrast, serves no one but himself and his own desire for domination. Doreen Irvine testifies to this when she describes how she gained prominence among the Satanist groups: she was able to demonstrate more feats of power than her rivals. The question of service, she says, never entered her head. She states that the first glimmer of there being something wrong with her life came when she realized that she was not able to exercise control over a Christian minister who had withstood her. This was a complete shock to her.[1]

There is, then, an immediate contrast between occult power and Christian power. The former binds people to the will of others; it is a power that enslaves. The Christian is given power to set captives free, as Jesus demonstrated in his own ministry.

This contrast alone ought to give us a strong clue to the origin of occult power.

Fascination with the Supernatural

Some people seem to be attracted by the unusual. They can be found not only in the ranks of the occult but also in those churches which emphasize and expect supernatural powers to be demonstrated in their meetings. Such people do not necessarily wish to learn anything about God or to grow in holiness of life; they are just attracted by occurrences out of the ordinary. The New Testament has such a character on record in Simon the magician, who wanted to receive the gift of the Spirit and the ability to pass "it" on to others. He was severely rebuked by Peter (Acts 8:9-25).

The various phenomena of occult meetings provide such people with a degree of meaning and fulfillment. Such demonstrations of power become like a drug on which they begin to depend. As a consequence, they become gullible and easily manipulated.

A Spiritually Impotent Church

Many, by contrast, have looked for a real spiritual experience within the church but have been disillusioned by its liberalism and unbelief. They begin to search elsewhere and are attracted to the occult with its demonstrations of spiritual power.

When I became minister of one church, I learned that a choir member had been healed through going to a spiritist medium. As the information had come to me indirectly, I felt unable to challenge the person directly, and so I brought the matter to God in prayer. Some time later I was preaching on the subject of Christian healing and incorporated into the service the testimony of a Christian woman in the church who had been healed of a heart condition. The choir member's response was to say that nobody in church these days really believes that Jesus still heals even if he did so in the past. He was expressing the church's lack of faith, which had prompted him to consult the medium when he needed healing. He could not accept that Jesus was able to heal in his church. Perhaps this was partly because he was under conviction for having gone outside the church for prayer with a view to healing.

The Western church, however, can learn much from its missionaries working in Third World countries that have no difficulty in perceiving a spiritual struggle in which evil spirits are active. Frank Vaughan, a Baptist missionary working in Brazil, reports how he first had to overcome his Western skepticism regarding the reality of evil spirits before he could properly minister. When he encountered widespread spiritism, he found that healing came only when Christians prayed with authority in the name of Jesus. He tells of a disturbance during a birthday party following an evangelistic service:

> A woman asked us to pray for a 7-year-old girl. Neuza was subject to "attacks" of "epilepsy." She had spasms of laughter or crying, after which she collapsed and slept for two or three days. These attacks had increased to once or twice a week. She had had all the medical treatment available, including psychiatry, to no avail. Her mother was desperate. There and then a small group of us prayed for the girl, claiming healing and cleansing in the name of Jesus Christ. She was wonderfully healed with no recurrence of the problem. Praise the Lord![2]

At the Lausanne Conference, a missionary reported that many of his colleagues in the Arctic came under demonic activity and apprehension with which they could not cope and, as a consequence, left that particular sphere of work. This resulted in a training-and-preparation program being set up so that, whether the missionaries-to-be accepted the existence of the demonic or not, they would at least be prepared when confronted by it.

The mission field has much to teach the church at home concerning the reality of evil spiritual forces and their overthrow when confronted by the power of Christ.

The Bankruptcy of Materialism

In the 1970s Billy Graham said that we were living in the time of the seeking generations.[3] People with material wealth and security had become starved of spiritual reality. They were seeking meaning but were not, in general, looking in the direction of the Christian church. We all know about the hippies and the "flower children" and the growth of experiments in communal living and alternative lifestyles in the mid-1960s. But many are still reverting to forms of paganism dating from pre-Christian times. Every year at the time of the summer solstice in Britain, hundreds of young people trek to Stonehenge on Salisbury Plain to witness the ancient Druidic rite of welcoming the sun back to his world. Then they perform their own rite, a hodge-podge of ancient rituals with modern chants and songs.

In the 1980s and 1990s the pendulum has swung in the opposite direction with the yuppie generation. By contrast with young people in the 1960s, yuppies are not rejecting the materialistic standards of the day but seeking to advance their own careers, make money and accumulate possessions. Richard Foster was thinking of the yuppie quest for personal power when he wrote: "Power destroys relationships. Lifelong friends can turn into mortal enemies the moment the vice-presidency of the company is at stake. Climb, push, shove, is the language of power."[4]

For many, however, the pace of such living offers no fulfillment, and so they start to look for a spiritual center for their
lives. This need for a spiritual center is clearly the force behind
the rise in "new age" religions. The real genius of this "new age"
religion is its ability to incorporate (or syncretize) a number of
different Eastern and Western influences, such as Aztec and
Mayan beliefs, traditional Buddhism, modern psychology (especially Jungian psychology), ancient pagan rituals and magic,
and, in some cases, mystical Christian spirituality. Though dismissed by some as the "moronic convergence" or "a national
fruit-loops day," the so-called harmonic convergence did, at
least, demonstrate the popularity and influence of the "new
agers."

Occult Power and Deception

Many people have found that, for them, the occult works. There
is a modern creed that states, "If it is real then it must be right."

> Bill Johnstone of South Shields lost contact with his father
> when his father went away to sea. The relations thought that
> the father had either died or emigrated to Australia. Bill at-
> tended a Ouija session and, like so many others, "imagined
> they were pushing the glass from one letter to another. . . .
> I asked the spirit if he knew where my father was. Back came
> the message—Dumfries, Scotland." Enquiries of Dumfries
> Council revealed that a Mr Bryce Johnstone was there and
> living at Alderman Hill Road. When father and son met,
> father said, "No-one in South Shields could have known
> where I was. Bill was a baby when I last saw him."[5]

This kind of testimony can be multiplied many times over. But
does the fact that the occult works make it all right? In a tel-

evision series entitled "Alternative Medicine," a young man was
featured who had become aware of his ability to heal. He was
not particularly religious nor had his experience brought him to
faith. He accepted his ability as a natural gift or power which
he was willing to use. The program concentrated on his clinic,
to which people came for sessions of healing with the laying on
of hands—for a fee. No prayers of any kind were offered. The
program showed a number of people who testified to receiving
help and healing in instances where medical professionals had
failed. This man has access to some kind of power that works.
But does that make it all right?

Some years ago my wife and I were taking our baby daughter
for a walk in a park. We asked an elderly lady if she would mind
taking our camera and photographing us as a family group. She
very kindly obliged and we soon struck up a friendship. She
invited us to her house near the park for a cup of tea. When
we told her that we were involved in Christian ministry in a
local evangelical church, she told us about her own healing
experience.

She had once accidentally pushed a needle straight into her
eye. Immediately she rang her nearest "practitioner." She did
not mean a general practitioner but one of the recognized
healers belonging to the Christian Science organization. "He
simply put his open palm in front of my eye, closed his eyes and
then slowly drew away his hand. The needle came out of my eye
and seemed to stick straight into his hand. I felt no pain whatsoever."

The lady seemed so pleasant and friendly; surely her healing
was all right? She later attended a Christian meeting and became greatly agitated at the mention of the fact that we are
sinners and need to be born again. It seemed that despite her

"religious" experience of healing, she was no nearer to knowing Jesus after it than before. If anything, she seemed unable to open her heart to the gospel message of God's saving love for her.

Then there is the uncanny relevance of much of the material allegedly given by departed loved ones in spiritist séances. Ralph Gasson was a spiritist medium of some note before his conversion to Christianity. He describes his experiences as a medium:

> I had a spirit guide who claimed to be an African witchdoctor stating that he had been in the spirit world for 600 years. . . . I was considered very fortunate by other envious students when I went into a deep trance and was controlled by my African guide at my first sitting. . . . A man sitting in that same circle who also understood the African dialect conversed quite naturally with the spirit who was controlling me and interpreted what was being said into English. I myself have never known a word of any African dialect. The reader must make no mistake about it, the spirit power is real and not just mere hallucination.[6]

Now is the time to remind ourselves of the Bible's caution about testing the spirits to see whether they are from God. The Bible goes on to say that every true and acceptable spiritual activity should exalt the truth that Jesus Christ has come in the flesh. This is plainly not the effect of most of the occult phenomena we have been discussing.

Whatever the reasons why people are attracted to the occult, many discover its power to be real. Because the occult works for them, we now need to ask whether its power is from God or whether it is a deception.

6

Why the Occult Works

Occult power is real and effective. We must now look at some of its possible sources to see if it comes from God. When the occult works, is it just by chance? Is it a trick? Is it due to natural psychic powers or external intelligence or the spirits of the departed? Or is there another source?

Chance

Sometimes a horoscope, for instance, may seem extraordinarily relevant to one's situation. A great deal of the material is fairly ordinary and unspecific, and enquirers can read into it the significance they need for guidance and reassurance. Sometimes things "just happen," and we must accept that it is simply coincidence and leave it there. No particular "power" is necessarily at work when such coincidences occur.

Fraud

Some occult practitioners, astute observers of human character, adjust their material to suit their clients and so manipulate them to some extent. Others are quite fraudulent, such as the company which purported to sell occult charms with proven success, quoting the names of satisfied customers. Television emcee Esther Rantzen and her team contacted some of these customers and found them all to be employees of the company concerned! I think it only fair to say in passing that the standard spiritist organizations, such as the National Spiritualist Union, are glad to expose fake practitioners.

Telepathic or Psychic Powers

There is a growing scientific interest in telepathy and psychic powers. As Christians we must accept that some people are capable of psychic activity. Whether they are to be encouraged in this direction is another matter.

Michael Perry says that the proper reaction to psychic forces is to offer them to God. He applies Paul's warning—that the love of money is the root of evil—to psychic experience. Beware of loving it; it is evil.[1] He also points out that it is a mistake to regard the psychic as spiritual. Such endowments cannot come from the Holy Spirit or God, for they do not increase our spiritual growth or deepen our relationship with Jesus Christ. The psychic world is a gray area; it is best to give it over to God.

A growing number of psychiatrists and counselors point out that the long-term effects of psychic experimentation can include the break-up of a person's wholeness and emotional and mental integration.

At the age of seventeen I discovered I had some telepathic ability. I could read people's thoughts quite accurately sometimes. After I had been converted, this ability remained, but I now felt quite ill at ease about it. After discussion and prayer I decided to offer the ability to God and renounce it. I was never again able to read people's minds and felt quite relieved, as I found it a burden more than a blessing.

External Intelligence

We have already mentioned that many sensitives or mediums claim to be guided by spirit powers. Doris Stokes claimed that superior intelligences gave her guidance and information. She was referring to spirit powers other than angels and demons, divinities other than the Trinity. Some suggest that external intelligence—possibly intelligences from other worlds—is the only real explanation for the phenomenon of the Ouija board; in a group setting it would be difficult for a player to manipulate the glass.

From a Christian perspective, this concept of external intelligence is unacceptable. We believe that God has made provision for our well-being through the Holy Spirit, who makes real to us the ministry and person of Jesus Christ. And although a few mediums claim to have the Holy Spirit as their guide, closer examination reveals that they use the term only as a label for the power that uses them. This is certainly not consistent with Scripture. A major role of the Holy Spirit is to exalt Jesus Christ as Lord. Because mediums do not do this, we can certainly doubt their claims to be guided by the Holy Spirit.

Departed Spirits

Most recipients of messages at séances say they have heard from a departed loved one or from some historical personage. For a great many, the information given is quite personal and seemingly knowable only by the departed person who, it is claimed, was communicating through the medium.

One spiritist I knew claimed that his spirit guide was Francis of Assisi. This guide did not, however, lead my friend in a lifestyle remotely similar to that of Francis; in fact, my friend said his guide told him that drug-taking and promiscuous sex were the new fruits of the Spirit! In this matter of messages from the departed, again, the test is whether these communications exalt Jesus Christ and reflect the holiness of God.

Where Do These Powers Come From?

Before we examine the Christian understanding of the source of the powers involved in the occult world, we must make a number of observations.

First, it is apparent and true that real powerful forces are at work. Chance and fraud do not explain most of the phenomena.

Second, some claim that these forces are benign and come from God, whether through supernatural powers or through the departed spirits of gifted people or deceased relatives. But if these forces were from God, they would encourage people to know the Lord Jesus Christ as Savior and to be part of his church. Despite the claims of many occult practitioners to be Christians, they lack commitment to the Christian gospel and are normally absent from the recognized Christian churches. The Bible plainly tells us that the gifts of God's Spirit are for the upbuilding of the common life of the church of Jesus (1 Cor 12:7,12-30). This same Bible passage also warns against other spirits which seek to lead people astray.

If these practices were from God, they would do us good. As James tells us in his letter, God's gifts are good and perfect (Jas 1:17). But the occult has become a snare for many people who have needed to be set free by Jesus. Such practices hinder spiritual growth and development.

Third, some see occult powers as neutral psychic forces from within the individual. Neutral they cannot be. From a Christian perspective, every gift and talent we have must be surrendered to God for his blessing and use so that his name may be glorified and his kingdom extended. Such occult abilities actually promote a sense of independence from God, reflecting the old sin of Adam who rebelled against God and refused to follow his laws. Behind such attitudes is the master of deception himself, whom Jesus described as a liar from the beginning (John 8:44). People who have psychic abilities must offer them to God and begin to discover the spiritual resource which God has certainly sanctioned, his own Holy Spirit.

Finally, there is no getting away from the fact that the Bible condemns occult practices.[2] This confirms that occult powers are not from God.

So where do they come from?

The Demonic

The only conclusion a Christian can draw is that occult phenomena are demonic in origin. These verses from the Old Testament are typical of the Bible's viewpoint:

> When you enter the land the LORD your God is giving you, do not learn to imitate the detestable ways of the nations there. Let no one be found among you who sacrifices his son or daughter in the fire, who practices divination or sorcery, interprets omens, engages in witchcraft, or casts spells, or who is a medium or spiritist or who consults the dead. Anyone who does these things is detestable to the LORD, and because of these detestable practices the LORD your God will

drive out those nations before you. You must be blameless
before the LORD your God. (Deut 18:9-13)

Add to this the account of Saul's death because of his lack of
trust in God evidenced by his consultation with a medium (1
Chron 10:13-14). What God forbids is not only contrary to his
nature but harmful for us as well. It follows that such phenomena have their origin in evil. The Bible does not allow for or
allude to any other possible source.

Evil Spirits

There are a number of passages in the Bible which confirm that
the demonic world is behind occult phenomena. In Philippi,
Paul encountered a woman with a gift of divination. She followed Paul and his colleagues, crying, "These men are servants
of the Most High God, who are telling you the way to be saved."
What this woman proclaimed was quite accurate, but there was
something wrong. The account tells us that she had a spirit by
which she predicted the future. It does not say that she had a
gift of the Holy Spirit or an innate ability. When Paul responded to the situation, he addressed the spirit inside her with
the words: "In the name of Jesus Christ I command you to come
out of her!" (Acts 16:16-18).

There was no debate or discussion, only a straight command
to the spirit to leave the woman. This happened immediately
and, in consequence, she was no longer able to prophesy. It is
clear that this ability to predict the future accurately was due
to the presence of a demonic spirit of divination in the woman.

Another illustration of the demonic origin of occult practice
can be seen in Acts 19 where Paul extends his mission to Ephesus. In response to the victory of Christ over the demonic world,
a number of those involved in sorcery were so challenged and

disturbed that they gave up all their occult books and burned them publicly. The New Testament church did not regard the occult as neutral—and certainly not as divine in origin. The effect of the gospel is to deliver people from its grasp.

The Bible is very clear about the influence of evil spirits in people's lives. We are told that before we were converted to Christ we were "children of disobedience" ruled by the demonic spirit of the air.[3] The apostle John describes the fallen world in general as being "under the control of the evil one" (1 Jn 5:19). The New Testament speaks of evil spirits as fallen angels. Revelation 12:7, for example, tells us that Satan and his angels fought a losing battle in heaven and were cast down on to the earth.[4] As the world draws to a close before the return of Christ, Satan himself will perform signs and wonders (2 Thess 2:9).

Satan and his evil spirits are real personalities and not just impersonal influences. They can speak; they believe, but tremble.[5] They can exercise their wills, and they seem to know that the Lordship of Jesus means that their time of rule will come to an end.[6] A man called Legion cried out to Jesus: "What do you want with me, Jesus, Son of the Most High God? I beg you, don't torture me!" (Lk 8:28). Their ability to recognize the divine person of Jesus reveals that they are intelligent beings.

Communicating with the Departed

One of the Bible's basic teachings relating to life after death is that there is to be no direct communication from the dead to the living. When King Saul desperately sought guidance from a medium concerning a forthcoming battle, did he encounter the real Samuel or not? Some have argued that if he did, the Bible seems to approve of spiritism. According to the medium herself, it *was* the real Samuel, and she was afraid. It is apparent that the woman was not expecting the *real* Samuel, and she supposed that her visitor had deceived her (1 Sam 28:8-12).

Some use this passage to argue that it is acceptable to consult the dead, who really do appear. Yet this case differs from that of a medium in a trance state, overtaken by a spirit guide. First, the fact that the real Samuel appeared tells us that the manifestation was not that of the spirit guide which usually operated through the medium. Samuel spoke independently of the woman's powers and was not under her control. Secondly, the enterprise was conducted in secrecy, because spiritism is wrong in the eyes of the Lord and the biblical punishment was death. Even the disturbed Samuel reminded Saul that what he was doing was forbidden, and so this story cannot be used to encourage spiritism at all. It in fact condemns spiritism, and Saul and his family paid a high price for their disobedience.

But the appearance of the real Samuel does raise questions about the return of the dead to the earth. Christians may need to be cautiously open here, saying that God in his sovereignty allowed the real Samuel to return and act as his prophetic messenger to condemn Saul for his occult practices when the king should have been relying upon God for guidance.

Then we have the account of the appearance of Elijah and Moses with Jesus at the transfiguration (Mk 9:2-8). Was this a purely mystical experience, or was this a real flesh and blood encounter? Again, we notice some striking differences from the spiritistic norm.

First, no medium called forth Elijah and Moses; it was the Lord of life himself, Jesus Christ. Jesus took the initiative for purposes of his own; there was no medium on a human quest for knowledge and guidance. Second, the conversation of Elijah and Moses was with Jesus alone and not with other people. This is the only occasion when Jesus is recorded as meeting with "the departed" and must be accepted as a unique event for a particular purpose known only to the Lord himself. Third, contact between the disciples and Elijah and Moses was discouraged. Peter wanted to build tabernacles for all three to dwell in, but God brought down a cloud and challenged the disciples to concentrate on knowing Jesus and to listen to him. Moses and Elijah did not continue to associate with the living; they simply disappeared from view.

This may seem to suggest that what happened was a vision, but the facts do not bear this out. The disciples saw Jesus, who was no vision, talking to these great men from the Old Testament period. Again, the appearance of these two prophets in no way encourages spiritism, for no occult encounter took place. The transfiguration was a unique and unrepeatable supernatural event.

Spiritistic claims directly contradict the Bible. It is in fact demonic spirits, impersonating the dead, who communicate with the living. The apostle Paul wrote: "Our struggle is not against flesh and blood, but against the rulers, against the authorities, against the powers of this dark world and against the spiritual forces of evil in the heavenly realms" (Eph 6:12).

Some Bible commentators say that this text gives us an insight into the organized nature of evil and that we have here a list of evil powers in descending order of power. Ralph Gasson says that it is the devil's counterfeit of God's order of power and authority among the angelic hosts—archangels and then angels under the divine rule of God. Regardless, we can say that most if not all occult activity to some degree counterfeits the spiritual gifts and powers that God has offered to his church through his Holy Spirit.[7]

Elsewhere, Paul describes the rituals of pagan worship, and in particular the worship of idols. He says that the mind behind such practices is demonic: "The sacrifices of pagans are offered to demons, not to God" (1 Cor 10:20). He also warns: "The Spirit clearly says that in later times some will abandon the faith and follow deceiving spirits and things taught by demons" (1 Tim 4:1). I do not think that it is stretching a point to say that this verse, and others like it, point to the various cults which have developed as pseudo-Christianity, as well as to other occult practices we have been discussing. Michael Harper speaks of this proliferation of religious deviations as "the devil's Pentecost." As Christians we should be warned that the occult is a real attempt by the evil one to produce an alternative to Christianity.

Occult involvement feeds idolatry by concentrating attention on one's own abilities and not on the one true God who has revealed himself uniquely through his Son, Jesus Christ our Lord. The first evil temptation in the Garden of Eden was the false promise that "ye shall be as gods" (Gen 3:5 KJV). Ever since, humanity has been trying to save itself and failing miserably.

Occult power is evil. It forms part of the strategy of our adversary the devil to keep men and women in spiritual bondage. Occult involvement, being typical of man's sinful rebellion against God's Word, brings people under spiritual domination. We shall now look at the nature of that evil domination and then see how Jesus can set people free.

7

Signals of Distress: Discernment before Ministry

How does evil oppression manifest itself? What signs should we look for when called on to help those experiencing it? The indications of demonic activity are many. People may experience such phenomena as a sense of the continuing presence of a close relative who has recently died, noises and unexplained movements of objects in a house, personality changes after occult practices, an inordinate fear of death, distressing nightmares, anger or strong, unmanageable fears.

Of the many times when I have been asked to pray with somone for release from evil spirits, only about a third actually needed to be set free from evil oppression. The others had equally genuine needs but they were not demonic in origin; they ranged from emotional hurts to obsession with evil, from long-standing guilt and mental disturbances to plain disobedience to the Word of God. I never begin a counseling situation with the assumption that a person will need deliverance from evil spirits, even if such is their claim. Such an assumption is not very helpful and, in some cases, can be harmful.

Counseling before Ministry

It is important to gather all the relevant information we can before deciding on the form of ministry to offer. A good principle to maintain is "counseling before ministry." Counseling helps to clarify the issues, and doing so will suggest what kind of ministry will be appropriate—whether deliverance or some other form of prayer and care.

As a good approach to counseling, I would recommend the chapter entitled "Counsel for the Counselors" in *Deliverance,* edited by Michael Perry. The chapter strongly advocates open-hearted listening, in which the helper does not jump in too early with his or her own interpretations of the problem. As we listen, we also listen to God, and can make it our inward prayer to be guided and protected by Jesus. As we listen, we should make notes of all the relevant information, including any social and domestic history, and any medical information which may shed light on the person's state of health and mind. All this is good discipline, and may help us to avoid rash conclusions. Far too many people have been hurt by ministry which has been too hastily and lazily begun.

After that preliminary word of caution, we shall now turn to look at some symptoms which may alert us to the presence of an evil influence.

Poltergeists

I was once approached by a minister who asked me to cleanse

a house of poltergeist activity. The word *poltergeist* is generally used to refer to alleged spirits who make their presence felt by making noises or moving objects. The minister had come across this problem after he had been asked to baptize the two children of a couple who lived in the house. The parents were not Christians, but out of fear they had asked him to get rid of the spirit in the house.

Most counselors say that the source of a poltergeist is not a spirit but, rather, the inner distress and tension within certain people, usually young children before the age of puberty. It often reflects anxieties in personal relationships which cause them pain. How this actually works is still a mystery, but with the release of stress, the phenomena usually cease.

My minister friend was anticipating an exorcism of some kind and wanted support. But I wanted first to listen to the couple and check out their story. They mentioned a number of experiences, such as feeling a "presence" at the top of the stairs, hearing noises around the house and noticing that the television had been moved from its normal place in the living room without actually seeing it happen. The couple were in considerable fear. My friend and I did not sense anything particularly odd about the atmosphere in the house, and we understood that the couple had not personally witnessed anything themselves.

As we continued to ask questions, we discovered that the man of the house had in fact two women living with him, neither of whom he had married. The two small children each had a different mother. It was then that I suggested we pray with the children, who were upstairs. One of the women accompanied us, and the children both looked strained and tense. I asked them how they felt about their home and they said they felt sad.

Laying our hands on them we prayed that they might know the love, peace and care of Jesus in their hearts. We made an appointment to return a week later and left.

When we returned, we found that the parents had noticed no further activity or disturbance. We also observed that the children seemed happier. At this stage we offered some pastoral advice on the family's need for a secure home without the many tensions which their lifestyle presented. The man replied that since we had prayed in the home, one of the women had decided to return to her own husband and that she had taken her son with her.

This underlines the importance of listening to all the relevant information before proceeding with any ministry. That household did not need deliverance, but a change in lifestyle and more wholesome morals within the home. Having made these changes, they had no further disturbances in the house.

Sometimes we are asked to exercise deliverance ministry when counsel alone is sufficient; at other times we are asked to counsel when deliverance is what is needed.

As we look at some of the forms of distress which are often brought for counsel and healing, let us watch for signals indicating that deliverance ministry is necessary. I hasten to add that these signals are only indicators of the presence of evil within a person; they are not conclusive evidence.

Mental and Emotional Problems

A question often raised is "How do you know that this person is not emotionally or mentally disturbed?" We must examine some common symptoms of mental and emotional illness and see how they are to be distinguished from demonic manifestations.

Possession Syndrome

Some psychiatrists speak of the "possession syndrome." This is a symptom of various disorders, the most common of which is schizophrenia. This illness is characterized by delusional thinking, hallucinations, and a sense of being controlled and acted on by alien forces which the sufferer sometimes understands to be demons.

There are also various neurotic illnesses, such as the hysterical personality disorder, in which the individual, often craving attention, adopts the symptoms of possession in order to secure it. Such accounts are usually embellished according to the person's understanding of what it means to be possessed! Excessive descriptions should alert the counselor to the possibility that this may be a case of mental illness. Before proceeding with any ministry, it is only wise to ask permission to consult the sufferer's doctor or psychiatrist, if he or she has been receiving treatment.

Most psychiatrists who accept the reality of spiritual warfare find it difficult to distinguish between demonic symptoms and evidence of a mental or emotional illness. It is quite true that many of the manifestations of possession, such as speaking in a different voice (that voice speaking as if it were a separate entity within the person) and sudden bursts of great strength, could be accounted for by mental illness.

Most seem to think that a fearful reaction to the things of God, especially the name of Jesus, strongly indicates the presence of an evil spirit. Kurt Koch says that when he has prayed with the mentally ill, there was a stillness and a passivity when the name of Jesus was mentioned. If the illness was demonic there was usually quite a noticeable reaction.[1]

A second indicator of demonic activity is behavior out of

keeping with the person's known personality or with recognized pathological states. Doctor William Wilson has a more pragmatic approach to distinguishing the demonic from an illness. He says that where possessionlike manifestations occur, and psychiatric treatment has failed to alleviate them or to give the individual a measure of control, then it is time for deliverance ministry. He goes so far as to say that in many of the mental hospitals whose patients are labeled as chronic schizophrenics or depressives, there has been healing through prayers of deliverance, sometimes without the patient's permission and sometimes in their absence.[2]

The Bible offers no hard and fast guidelines on how one determines whether a demon is present. In the Gospels, some manifestations of the demonic occurred due simply to the presence of Jesus. The only other clue is the reference to the discerning of spirits in the list of charismatic gifts in 1 Corinthians 12. The verb here means "discriminate" and can refer not just to the spiritual world but also to the motives behind human activities. Paul himself seems to have exercised this gift when he cast out an unclean spirit from a medium who was harassing him in Philippi (Acts 16:16-18).

We need to recognize our limitations in this area and consult other professionals when appropriate. If psychiatric help has not brought healing, we may conclude that deliverance prayer is necessary. Many ministers can testify to being approached by staff from psychiatric units and being asked to pray for a patient because what he or she really needed was spiritual help.[3]

Projection
Some apparently healthy individuals may find aspects of their lives and personalities undesirable. These aspects are usually

repressed. In times of stress they may surface and somehow take the form of hostile external forces. As in possession syndrome, the sufferer's internal anxieties are being projected outside himself or herself and given the status of spirits at work. This is the individual's often unconscious attempt to maintain some balance.

For example, there may be deep feelings of anger and hurt through being rejected as a child. These feelings are stored up inside. Later, rather than directing them at the people who may be responsible for the hurt, the person transforms them, as it were, into the form of spirits within. The original anger still needs to be dealt with. In these cases, prayer for deliverance may temporarily help to remove the anxiety, but it will not solve the problem. The individual needs to confront and deal with his or her emotions.

Not long ago, a counselor asked me to join him in ministering to a woman who had already received some deliverance ministry but still needed help. When she arrived she immediately produced a long list of the spirits which she had identified as being within her. There must have been well over 150 names on that list, ranging from anger and hatred to laziness, lying and depression. It listed all kinds of conditions which any normal person experiences from time to time.

As she told us her story, she happened to mention that she did not get on too well with her mother although she loved her. She repeated this a number of times, almost always with some criticism of her mother. So I asked her to relax in her chair and close her eyes. I briefly thanked Jesus that he was with us as we were all Christians, and I prayed that he would guide the work we were about to share. Then I asked her to imagine her mother (who is still alive) opening the door and walking into the room.

The woman stiffened, her breathing became excited and she shrieked in anxiety. She became like a little girl cowering in a corner for fear of some dread punishment. I encouraged her to realize that what she was feeling was not some spirit in the room, but the coming to the surface of these long-repressed fears. I also encouraged her to stay in touch with the fact that she was a child of God and by his grace was free to make decisions for herself.

Then I asked her what she would like to say to her mother. With a little help she eventually said, quite strongly, "Mother, get off my back. I'm going to live my own life with the help of Jesus." All her life her mother had dominated her and had been quite hard with her. She was afraid to face up to her mother and express her feelings and, so, had convinced herself that some evil spirits had taken hold of her.

Demonic Oppression

Having said all this, we must also acknowledge that evil spirits can gain a hold over our hurt feelings and damaged minds. When counsel and help of whatever kind have been offered, but to no avail, we may have to conclude that the person needs to be freed from the influence of an evil spirit. Some of the emotions which may indicate that this is at the root of the problem are hatred, anger, fears of various kinds, pride, self-pity and rejection. (I am not speaking of those moments when any of us may lose our temper or feel hurt. Those are emotions which come and soon go because we do not nurse them or brood on them.) If we have dealt with the hurt which may account for the initial experience of any of these emotions, yet the feelings seem fixed or locked in the person's life, then it is likely that the authority of Jesus is needed to deliver him or her from evil.

Should any of the emotional distress relate to occult involvement, this too strongly indicates the need for deliverance. We should check to see where these feelings come from and work through them to find healing. If the person continues to be bound by them, a simple prayer for freedom may be necessary. (In chapter ten, there is a standard prayer for deliverance which the counselor can use.)

Some time ago a woman came to see me. She belonged to an evangelical fellowship which encouraged the exercise of spiritual gifts. The problem worrying her was that, during corporate praise and worship, she had a terrific urge to pray in tongues at the top of her voice so that everyone could admire how gifted she was. She had prayed much about this and asked God to forgive her and help her to be more humble. But the problem persisted for many years. She felt that her Christianity was being fought out over this one issue.

As we gathered information from her past in order to help us understand the situation, she mentioned that only once in her life had she had the opportunity to take center stage, and that was as a child in a school play. She replaced the leading lady and greatly enjoyed herself. But during the applause at the end of the performance, she felt a strong rush of pride, which she fostered. It was this same feeling which caused her difficulties in worship. After she repented of the pride she had taken on board that day at school, I prayed that the oppressing spirit and the pride would be broken and cast out. She coughed and shook a little, but she was soon free and she seemed to know it. Afterward she reported that she could enjoy worship without the old pride rising within her.

Our adversary the devil, in seeking to spoil lives through the agency of evil spirits, tries to gain a foothold in the area of unconfessed sin. When our feelings are damaged and hurt, we are tempted to brood over them and become bitter. We must learn to forgive others and confess to God our own need of forgiveness and healing. This is the advice Jesus gave to the man he healed at the pool of Bethesda. He told him to stop sinning or else matters would get worse (Jn 5:14).

Speech Problems

Speech problems can be another pointer to the need for deliverance. I do not mean problems such as stuttering or getting tongue-tied. I mean uncontrolled outbursts of verbal abuse, lying, cursing and blasphemy. These are often found among people who have belonged to sects which include the deliberate denouncing of Christian belief and blasphemy as part of their initiation rites.

When I was part of the Manchester Deliverance Advisory Group, we went through a phase of ministry in which a number of people were trying hard to break free of the black magic groups to which they had belonged. On many occasions those seeking help and deliverance spoke of strong attacks of verbal abuse within their minds, which caused them much distress. Freedom came with careful nurturing in their newfound Christian faith, coupled with repentance for what they had previously said about Jesus and his church.

Very often a helpful element in this process was to encourage them to say aloud what they now believed, to give verbal testimony to what the Lord Jesus Christ had done for them. I am reminded of those words in the book of Revelation which say that the Christian witnesses overcame the devil "by the blood of the Lamb and by the word of their testimony" (Rev 12:11).

This may sound rather simple but, as Paul says, once we

surrender parts of our bodies to sin, they become slaves to that sin. They individually need to be retrieved and cleansed from sinful use (Rom 6:16). So if the tongue, for instance, has been surrendered to evil, it needs to be re-surrendered to the glory of God. That is why I believe it is good practice, especially in the deliverance context, to confess aloud and then to praise God aloud. The Bible confirms the importance of the spoken word. God spoke creation into being; blessings spoken in faith could not be retrieved. We must not miss the spiritual importance of the spoken declaration. It is as we believe in our hearts and confess with our lips that we shall be saved (Rom 10:10).

When Jesus was confronted by people bothered by spirits, there were always outbursts. Sometimes, before Jesus had spoken, the tormenting spirit would cry out in fear, "What do you want with us, Jesus of Nazareth? Have you come to destroy us!" Such outbursts are usually signs of distress within the person and a reaction by the evil spirit to the authority of Christ present in the counselor. Should this happen during counseling we should prayerfully follow Jesus' example and command the spirit to be quiet and come out.

Let me emphasize again that we are not here referring to occasional outbursts of temper or occasional lies. The demonic phenomena are far more obsessive and aggressive than that. We should not conclude that we have given room to an evil spirit if we lose our temper one day. But we should certainly avoid making a habit of losing our temper or lying. This would be persistently to give place to sin and, if not checked, may result in giving room to an evil spirit.

Sexual Problems
Our sexuality is another aspect of our personalities in which

Satan may try to cause problems. He may play on recurring unclean sexual thoughts and fantasies, leading to masturbation, deepening lusts, perversions, homosexuality, fornication or incest. Of the twenty-nine references in the New Testament to encounters with demonic spirits, six refer to "evil" spirits and the remaining twenty-three to "unclean" spirits. The Greek word used here, *akathartos,* usually refers to moral uncleanness. We should not be surprised, then, that the manifestation of evil can include a sexual element.

Many covens and Satanist groups employ multiple sexual experiences as bonding elements within their groups (although some accounts are exaggerated). Audrey Harper, a former witch, mentioned in a televised interview that when she was initiated into a coven she was immediately required to have sexual intercourse. If she had objected, she said, she would have been forcibly raped. Such a destructive approach cannot but scar the sensibilities of the participants. Audrey Harper spent seventeen years undergoing psychiatric care before she was able to come to terms with life again.

Some years ago a Christian girl came for ministry, saying that she was having great difficulty breaking free from a lesbian lifestyle which she had practiced for a number of years. She had repeatedly prayed and received counsel, but there seemed to be a powerful compulsion at work within her against her will. She had repented of her former life and did not enjoy these feelings. She shared that some years earlier she had dabbled in the occult, playing with a Ouija board. Some time later she began her relationships with other women. Later still she became a committed Christian, but these nagging compulsions hindered her Christian growth.

After spending some time with her, I was convinced that she

truly desired to be free from her homosexual compulsions. I was also convinced that she was not constitutionally homosexual. So I prayed for her deliverance, commanding an unclean spirit to leave her alone and come out of her in the name of Jesus. In a couple of further interviews I encouraged her to adopt certain spiritual disciplines for her growth. She eventually found a church which helped her to settle down. She said that she felt refreshed and had been freed from her compulsive drives. She has remained free ever since.

Some readers may need to be reassured that not all difficulties in our sexual lives arise from a demonic presence. As Christians we are always striving to walk that narrow path with Jesus and avoid the temptations that focus on our physical and emotional passions. Some problems, such as masturbation, arise out of the natural curiosities that are part and parcel of growing up. They may reflect other tensions or feelings of sexual inadequacy and act as a self-indulgent release. But, like any abuse of our bodies, they can develop into a real bondage. In this way they can offer the demonic realm an entrance into our lives.

An evangelical lay pastor once told me about the time he was laid off from his secular job. He became extremely depressed, and fell into the habit of visiting local pornographic cinemas in the afternoon. This continued until he found another job. But the stimulation of the pornographic films led to the habit of masturbation. No matter how he tried to give up the habit, he could not. One day he realized that he was being oppressed by an unclean spirit, and immediately he commanded it to get out of his life. From that moment, he felt release and a new power in his life. From then on he was free from the domination of this habit.

This case history illustrates how this kind of domination can start during a particularly critical period or "life event." Victory over temptation can sometimes be hard won, but if we always lose we are not just tempted, we are dominated. In such instances, we need to trace the behavior back to its beginning. Then we must repent of it before God and ask Jesus to command that we be delivered from the unclean spirit.

Addictions

Sometimes, demonic influence lies behind compulsive addictions. We must exercise caution here; not every smoker, for instance, is demon-possessed! But sometimes there is a spiritual presence bound up in addictions to tobacco, alcohol, drugs and even overeating. Some people who have taken drugs such as cocaine and heroin will tell of great religious experiences. Some say that they have even been to heaven, while others have been terrified because they have seen the devil.

When I was a student, our supper was rudely interrupted one evening by a young man called Robby, who burst through the door saying he was going to die. He was obviously distressed, and I was asked to talk and pray with him. He had been a heroin addict since he was fourteen years old. I thought he was hallucinating under the influence of drugs. So after calming him down a little I prayed that the Lord would heal him of his addiction and come into his heart. He genuinely turned to Christ that night and recovered from his fear very quickly.

He then explained that since taking drugs he had been receiving guidance to worship Satan as the true lord of the universe. He had been doing this for about a year now. A number of us went to his house and helped him to destroy the materials he had been using to worship in this way. For about a week he was emotionally up and down, but we continued to pray that he would be delivered from all demonic influence. His condition did stabilize, and he has since sorted himself out and joined a local evangelical fellowship.

Similar stories could be told by people who repeatedly get drunk. In both alcoholism and drug addiction our normal self-control breaks down. This can open the way to influences from our baser inclinations. The tempter can thus gain a foothold. If we sow to the flesh we will reap destruction from the flesh (Gal 6:8 KJV). It seems that there is something intrinsically evil in the cycle of self-destructive habits. As Christians we need to pray, "Lead us not into temptation."

Physical Infirmities

It is clear from some of the New Testament passages that some physical conditions can be demonically based. Luke tells us of one occasion when Jesus was driving out "a demon that was mute" (Lk 11:14-15). The individual was mute, but when the demon had been cast out, the man could speak. We are not told anything of his background, but the fact that he spoke immediately after he had received deliverance probably indicates that he had lost the power of speech through becoming possessed.

A similar account in Mark's Gospel tells of a boy said to have been bothered by a spirit from childhood. Jesus addressed the evil spirit as a deaf and dumb spirit (Mk 9:25). Interestingly, though it was a dumb spirit, it came out of the boy quite noisily. Elsewhere there is mention of a blind and dumb spirit (Mt 12:22).

There is also a reference to a "spirit of infirmity" in the case of an afflicted woman being bent over so that she could not straighten up at all (Lk 13:11). Here there is no mention of an exorcism. Jesus simply commanded the woman to be set free from her infirmity, laying his hands on her. (This was not typical of Jesus' deliverance ministry.) It seems to illustrate demonic activity of a lesser degree, which did not require exorcism as such. This sort of activity could also have caused the fever in Peter's mother-in-law, which Jesus rebuked (Lk 4:38-39). The fact that Jesus is described as "healing" those who were oppressed by evil spirits could refer to this approach to deliverance.[4] Certain people, though not possessed, may suffer from illnesses caused by demonic influence.

Michael Harper tells the story of a Salvation Army officer who had been born blind and who was brought to a meeting at which Jean Darnall was ministering. A charismatic word of knowledge declared that the man's blindness was due to an evil spirit which had entered him at birth. He had been born in prison. His father was a criminal and his mother had conspired with him. Criminal or immoral activity can become a vehicle for demonic intrusion, and this was the case for this officer. Following a deliverance prayer by which a spirit was cast out of him, the man saw perfectly for the first time in his life.[5]

Once again, we must not assume that all illness is caused by demonic influence. Many of our physical ailments result from our lifestyle, and if we want to be healed we may have to change the way we live. A person who drinks to excess and develops liver problems must not think that a spirit is causing his liver failure. He needs to repent of his bad habit and endeavor to restore his health as far as possible. This applies too to some psychosomatic illnesses. If we are given to excessive worrying or bouts of anger, then we may pay for it with an ulcer. Some may need inner healing and help to improve their condition. Those who minister to them must exercise caution and discernment. We must look to God to supply us with the gifts of his

Spirit to help us make the right decisions on how to proceed.

Religious Spirits

Someone has said that the devil is religious. It is a fact that many thousands of people are attracted to cults and societies which deny basic scriptural truths about the deity of Jesus Christ and the way of salvation—opened up once and for all by the sacrifice of Jesus on the cross for our sins. The list ranges from Jehovah's Witnesses, Mormons, the Moonies (Unification Church) and Christian Science, to those which incorporate facets of Eastern mysticism or New Age thinking, such as the Hare Krishnas. In addition we have seen an explosion of occult-based religions and cults.

The ancient rites of some churches reflect the need for protection from the influence of evil and the importance of continually walking in God's light and truth. In the baptismal rites of the Anglican and Roman Catholic churches, candidates are invited to affirm publicly that they renounce evil and turn to Christ. A prayer toward the end of the service in *The Alternative Service Book* includes: "May almighty God deliver you from the powers of darkness, and lead you in the light and obedience of Christ."[6] This is an effective way of reminding newly committed Christians that they are to live under the power of Christ, who has set them free from all spiritual bondage.

Some years ago I took part in a series of meetings on "Life in the Spirit." Someone present believed that God was giving a word of knowledge concerning a woman who had asked for prayer: she should formally renounce her involvement with a pseudo-religious group which followed highly questionable moral practices and teachings. The woman was shocked and challenged, but again the invitation to renounce evil was sensitively given. She struggled as she stated that she did renounce evil. She later said that a real battle was taking place. But with the prayer and gentle encouragement of the group ministering to her, she was able to confess her sin to the Lord. Filled with the Spirit, she began to praise the Lord with evident joy. She made good progress in her newfound freedom, and she said it felt as if an inner confusion had been lifted.

When Paul wrote to Timothy he stated that false doctrines and the abandoning of the true faith which inevitably follows are, in part, due to the work of deceiving spirits (1 Tim 4:1). Paul felt so strongly about this that he cautioned Timothy to watch his life and doctrine closely, for our salvation depends on our keeping the faith as well as on the Lord's keeping us (1 Tim 4:16).

It is certain that what we believe affects the way we live. Almost a quarter of the New Testament is devoted to Christian conduct in the light of what we believe about Jesus. So, if we embrace destructive and deceitful doctrines, the way we live will be influenced by them. In my experience, people in this situation find that the battle rages around one decision: whether or not they will truly commit themselves to Jesus Christ as Savior and only Lord. It is the will to repent and turn to Christ that demonic forces try to influence. This is why counselors should invite such people openly to ask for the help of the Holy Spirit to bring them to repentance and faith. They can then pray that the Lord would break whatever bondage of the will there may be and free those concerned to give their hearts and lives truly to God.

Most people suffering spiritual bondage find it difficult to grow as Christians. They may be reluctant to pray and read the Bible. Worship and effective preaching may provoke them to undue criticism and antagonism. (I am not, of course, referring to styles of worship that may offend us.)

Some years ago, an elder of a church where I was ministering told me that he would be happier if I left the church and went elsewhere. When I asked why, he replied, "You keep going on and on about Jesus, and it gets under my skin; I don't like it!" A man well respected in the church, he went on to say that he had been feeling like this for years but did not know why. He seemed to understand the message of the gospel and said that he believed it.

Further questioning revealed that his wife and mother-in-law had been subscribing to spiritism alongside their churchgoing. He had reluctantly been drawn into the proceedings, which had often taken place in his house before his wife's mother had died. I asked him if he had ever repented of this and asked the Lord to cleanse him from its effects. He said he found it hard to do so, for when he tried to pray about it he became afraid. We then prayed for his forgiveness and release. Afterward he said that he felt a lot clearer about what he really believed and no longer squirmed when the gospel was preached in his church.

Pointers, Not Proof

A final cautionary reminder: Signals such as these are no more than *possible* indicators of demonic influence. We must not conclude that everyone with similar problems is under demonic influence. Rather, we should check all other possible causes, and only then go on to see whether place has been given to the evil one. If we do feel that the problem has a spiritual root, we need not be alarmed. Deliverance can take place without extravagant behavior on the part of those who minister or those who are ministered to.

In the next chapter, we shall consider how to approach deliverance ministry and look at some of the ways the enemy can gain a foothold in people's lives.

8

Preparing for
Ministry

Jesus' ministry is one of deliverance, and the church, in the
name of Jesus, is to continue his work. Now is the time to clarify
what we mean by the term *deliverance. Webster's New Colle-
giate Dictionary* defines *deliver* as "to set free, liberate, or rescue
. . . to hand over." The Greek word used in the New Testament
is *rhyomai,* which means both "rescue from" and "preserve from
harm." So a basic definition for our purposes is: "Deliverance
means being set free from the bondage of Satan."[1]

Deliverance and Exorcism

It is necessary to distinguish between exorcism and deliverance.
Exorcism is a specific act of binding and releasing, and it is
usually performed for a person who is believed to be possessed
by a nonhuman malevolent spirit. The term may also be used

for the spiritual cleansing of a place believed to be infested or affected by the demonic.

Deliverance ministry may involve this too, but this is not generally the case. Deliverance ministry is concerned with breaking the bondages which arise from sinful living, by which Satan can seek to establish a spiritual grip.

Exorcism is concerned with casting out evil spirits which have possessed the individual. Deliverance ministry is the prerogative of all Christians engaged in pastoral care, whereas exorcism is performed by those specially trained and equipped for this work. Deliverance must be seen as an aspect of the whole ministry of Christ and his church. It is a part of the healing ministry; therefore, it cannot and must not be exercised apart from repentance toward God and faith in Jesus Christ. John Richards says that "it is better to think of deliverance 'to God' rather than 'from the Devil.' "[2] He firmly notes that our ministry should be equally concerned with the ongoing spiritual walk of the one who has been delivered.

Conversion and Deliverance

In one sense every Christian experiences deliverance ministry when he or she is converted to Jesus as Savior and Lord. Paul, describing the "before and after" of conversion, says, "You were dead in your transgressions and sins, in which you used to live when you followed the ways of this world and of the ruler of the kingdom of the air . . . but . . . God made us alive with Christ" (Eph 2:1-2, 4-5). He also speaks of converted people as having been "rescued [by God] from the dominion of darkness and brought . . . into the kingdom of the Son he loves" (Col 1:13). The salvation experience is, then, an experience of deliverance!

On entering the kingdom of God through Jesus, however, the

Christian faces a continual spiritual battle. The initial experience of deliverance is only the beginning of an ongoing warfare.[3]

We must be careful to take a balanced view of this. The apostle is not implying that the Christian life is an unremitting and direct battle with evil spirits. By overemphasizing demonic activity we pay insufficient attention to sin as the basic problem of the human condition. Paul wrote about the Christian's spiritual armor after emphasizing the need to preserve Christian standards against the background of a fallen and corrupt society (Eph 4:1—6:4). He had earlier spoken of the spiritual forces at work behind the scenes (Eph 2:2-4). It was these forces which both orchestrated and maintained the effects of sin and the Fall. So when Paul spoke of "that day of evil," he was forewarning his readers of the times when it may be necessary to confront such powers more directly (Eph 6:13).

While mentioning the reality of evil spirits, Paul has much more to say about holiness of life as the proper standard for Christian living. In the Ephesian letter he challenges the individual and the church to maintain a continuous discipline of holy living; he does not call for daily deliverances!

Real as these demonic forces are, however, we must be careful not to assume that every non-Christian is demon-possessed. The Bible does teach that before becoming Christians our minds were darkened and that we followed the wicked ways of the dark ruler of this world (Eph 2:2; 5:8). Of course, this does not mean that every non-Christian is demon possessed. The Gospels are filled with the stories of people who came to a living faith in Jesus without needing to be exorcised of evil spirits. When people are converted and born again of the Holy Spirit, they are brought into a new life with Jesus. As the new life of the Spirit begins to grow, the dominating influence of the power of darkness and the effects of their former lifestyles are diminished. But this new life must be nurtured by fellowship, prayer and faithful obedience to the Word of God. However, in some rare cases, a person needs to be set free from bondage to an evil spirit, either as a prelude to conversion or when the Holy Spirit highlights it after conversion.

Possession and Demonic Influence

A word of warning before we go further. We need to be careful about using the word *possession*. The term is used far too loosely in some Christian circles and covers too wide a range of needs. Such indiscriminate use not only gives the subject an unhealthy and frightening image, but shows that we fail to understand what the Bible means when it talks about the presence of an evil spirit in a person's life.

The Greek word *daimonizomenos,* which most translations render "possessed by a demon," means "under demonic influence." It can describe a range of conditions. The severest is possession by one or more evil spirits, leaving the individual very little control over his or her own life. The clearest example of this is the man possessed by a "legion" of demons (Mk 5:9). But these instances are much less frequent than cases of individual demonic influence.

Some suggest that the influence exerted by evil spirits ranges from temptation through oppression to actual possession. An *oppressed* person, they say, is "distorted" through demonic attack, while a *possessed* person is "controlled" by evil spirits. Michael Ross-Watson points out that there is no scriptural warrant for this distinction between types of spiritual attack.[4] The Greek word for "oppress," he adds, means "tyrannize" (as in Acts 10:38 where Jesus is described as healing those who were oppressed of the devil).

It is, however, important to underline the range of difficulties produced by these spiritual attacks, for different degrees of ministry may be required. It is helpful to recognize that some people's problems are very serious and others are less so. Both are equally in need of healing.

Most people involved in deliverance ministry do, in fact, distinguish between exorcism and deliverance ministry. The former, in British Anglican and Roman Catholic churches, may be carried out only by licensed and recognized exorcists who work in close cooperation with their bishops and usually with their own Deliverance Advisory Committees. The ministry of deliverance, on the other hand, can be carried out by pastors and ministers in consultation with more experienced colleagues.

The free churches do not have such clearly defined rules for deliverance ministry. It is usually the responsibility of individual pastors and leaders to act as they think best. Most do consult senior colleagues when possible, and all are accountable to their governing bodies. Some make use of ministers' fraternals within the local Council of Churches. Some years ago a free-church minister invited a number of Anglicans to assist him with some deliverance ministry, as he could not get the help he needed within his immediate church fellowship. I am glad to say that this kind of interchurch cooperation is increasing and being more frequently used by local ministers.

In the remainder of this chapter I will try to offer guidance for ministers and other church leaders about this difficult dimension of Christian ministry.

How the Devil Attacks

If we take the prayer of Jesus seriously when it says "Lead us not into temptation, but deliver us from evil," we need to be alert to the ways in which our spiritual adversary, the devil, operates. The New Testament shows that spiritual attack can come in a number of different ways. The direct assault of the enemy is compared to the charge of a roaring lion (1 Pet 5:8). Paul described his thorn in the flesh as a messenger of Satan (2 Cor 12:7). Many Christians believe that if our faith were strong we would not suffer such attacks. So it is encouraging to remind ourselves that this kind of assault befell even Paul, a man of great faith.

The devil operates more indirectly when we store up resentment or an unforgiving attitude whereby our fellowship with Jesus and his church is broken (2 Cor 10—11). Michael Harper describes this as a kind of siege by which our enemy seeks to gain entrance.[5] Another slippery and seductive tactic is the promotion of heresy, which inevitably leads to a false Christ or questionable morals. No wonder John taught us to "test the spirits to see whether they are from God" (1 Jn 4:1).

Then there is the more serious situation, caused when an evil spirit takes up residence within a person. Jesus himself used this picture on more than one occasion. He said that when seeking to set a person free or to win a spiritual battle, it is first necessary to bind the strong man of the house before one can enter in and claim the spoils for Christ (Mt 12:22-29). Jesus said that once a person was delivered it was vital for that person to dedicate that newly won "home" to God, lest an enemy far worse than before come and reside there (Mt 12:43-45).

The only New Testament example of anyone opening himself up to the devil in this way is that of Judas Iscariot. Significantly it happened when he deliberately and deceitfully sought to kill Jesus.[6] This condition is not the norm and is impossible for Christians who have come under the lordship of Jesus Christ.

But all of us, from time to time and in varying degrees, come under the influence of the demonic. The most common form of attack for Christians is temptation. Temptation itself is not a sin, but it is an attack on us. Even Jesus needed ministry after his battles with temptation in the desert. After his ordeal he needed the ministry of angels to renew him (Mt 4:11). This underlines the fact that temptation is a demonic attack. We need time to renew and refresh ourselves if we have been going through a particularly fierce battle.

Some Christians find it difficult to accept the unpleasant fact that *Christians* may need deliverance ministry. But this should not surprise us, since Jesus encountered the evil one in the synagogue itself. On one occasion, Jesus came across a man with an unclean spirit who was worshiping alongside everyone else (Mk 1:23). We might ask: "How often had the man been going to the synagogue before his encounter with Jesus drew forth the demon within him?"

Again, Peter once tried to steer Jesus away from Calvary and even rebuked him when he spoke of his death. Jesus reprimanded him sternly with the words, "Get behind me, Satan! You are a stumbling block to me; you do not have in mind the things of God, but the things of men" (Mt 16:23). Peter allowed himself to come under the influence of the evil one. Elsewhere, Jesus picks this up and tells him, "Satan has asked to sift you as wheat. But I have prayed for you, Simon, that your faith may not fail" (Lk 22:31-32).

Let us look, then, at further ways in which demonic influence and the power of the evil one can gain access into Christians' lives.

Heredity and Family Background

In Exodus we are told that children shall be punished for the sins of their parents to the third and fourth generations (Ex 20:5). But Ezekiel teaches us that God now deals with each person individually and that children would not suffer God's punishment for the sins of their parents (Ezek 18:19-20). Taken together, these passages teach that each of us will stand before God as individuals and be judged according to how we have lived in the light of God's grace. Yet we are not immune from the effects of our immediate family life and past history.[7]

Some parents who have been involved with the occult pass on to their children the presence of evil spirits which entered and influenced them as a result of their occult interests. Michael Harper relates an experience of deliverance during a preaching tour in Britain by the American minister Dennis Bennett in 1965.

At the end of one meeting, people were invited to come forward for prayer. When Bennett laid his hands on the head of a minister, there was a sharp reaction. The man slipped from his chair and appeared to go into a coma. Later he was encouraged to go aside to talk and receive further prayer. He agreed that he needed deliverance from this evil and agreed to further prayer. The moment the name of Jesus was mentioned there was another reaction.

Taking authority over this evil in the name of Jesus, those who were ministering to him cast out the spirit. Within a few moments, the man was on his feet, delivered and free. His family had been involved in the occult at some earlier time, and he had not known this.[8]

Sometimes the presence of evil survives in a so-called family illness. (This is not the same thing at all as hereditary illnesses such as hemophilia and color blindness, which are medically documented.)

I was once asked to counsel and pray with a Christian who had continual back trouble and a range of sicknesses that could not be traced to any physical root. As we talked, she told me that, as far as she knew, her father had similar illnesses all his life. She was quite sure that her grandfather was exactly the same. We agreed to take a step of faith and command a spirit of infirmity to go from her in the name of Jesus. We joined together in a simple prayer, and she immediately felt a loosening in her shoulder muscles and down her spine. She later testified that she was freed from the persistent bouts of ill health and general weakness as well as her back trouble. She is still free as I write, a year later.

Some family illnesses can be emotional and mental in nature. Great care needs to be exercised to determine if there is a known organic root to the inherited illness before coming to the conclusion that it may be demonic, requiring repentance and then deliverance. (Incidentally, we should be cautious about concluding that an illness is demonic just because we do not happen to know the cause.)

I once counseled a man who persistently felt a hand on his head. He believed this feeling was connected with the difficulties he felt in his Christian life. As we talked, it came to light that his mother had been a practicing medium. On her deathbed she had laid hands on him and given him her blessing. He could not get free from this spiritual hold on his life until he repented of receiving his mother's "blessing" and her involvement with the occult. This enabled him to let go of his mother's spirit and opened him up to the cleansing and forgiveness of God.

Damaged Childhood

Very often, hurts received in childhood can affect us throughout our adult lives. At one conference at which I was speaking, a woman came forward for prayer during a communion service. She said she was deeply concerned about her hatred for her mother. Her hatred was affecting her marriage and her relationship with the rest of her family. She wanted to surrender the problem to the Lord Jesus.

Her upbringing was one of unrelieved rejection and hardship. With the passage of time, she had stored up inside herself feelings of hatred and bitterness. She openly confessed this to the Lord and refused to hold on to her hurt feelings toward her mother. As she was praying, she could feel the dominating presence of her mother in the room and it made her afraid. We agreed that an evil spirit had entered her feelings and thoughts on the back of her suffering, mimicking her mother's dominance. We rebuked the dominating spirit and commanded it to get out of her life in the name of Jesus, to whom she belonged. She shivered and then felt released. As we quietly reminded her of the power and authority of Jesus, she opened her heart. Filled with the Spirit, she began to praise the Lord. She said that for many years she had felt little joy and love, but now she felt renewed in her heart by the Holy Spirit.

We should recognize, then, that evil spirits can gain access to our lives through the emotional hurts we carry and which we often repress deep within us.

Other factors through which our spiritual enemy seeks to get hold of us are rejection, fear and incest. The hurts received through these can fester within us and the devil can take advantage of the emotional damage done. The child mentioned in Mark 9:14-29 seems to illustrate this problem. The boy exhibited symptoms similar to those of epilepsy. Jesus asked, "How long has he been like this?" The father replied that the evil spirit (a deaf and mute spirit, literally "unclean") had come upon him during his childhood. The symptoms then described denote a spirit bent on doing violence to the boy. We have no further information on his background, but we can suggest that some event or hurt during his childhood may have resulted in his spiritual bondage.

Some years ago, I had a meal with a couple who had recently become Christians. They asked me to say grace. As I began to pray, their six-year-old son began to create a fuss and became quite aggressive as I continued. They later told me that he was a bit highly strung and that he had always acted a little strangely. Later he came into a room where I was praying. Without asking anyone's permission, I held him tightly around his waist and prayed simply for deliverance, commanding the spirit to stop troubling him and to leave him. The response was quite undramatic; he seemed to go into a brief trance and then he became much brighter and more cheerful. He no longer showed his aggression and disturbing behavior during prayer, and he was able to give himself more fully to his family. Later, his father confided that, before they became Christians, he and his wife had frequently had violent arguments in front of their son ever since he was born.

We need to recognize, then, that hurts sustained in childhood, if allowed to fester, can often become the means by which an evil spirit may enter someone's life. It may upset our sensibilities to talk about an attack on a child by the demonic world, but we must remember that our spiritual enemy has no love for mankind. He is a liar and delights in attacking the vulnerable.

When counseling people who were sexually abused by their

parents or a family member, a feeling of anger and revulsion can often surface in them. Sometimes, despite offering counsel and care, these feelings seem impossible to dislodge. In fact, they often increase in strength when prayed over in the usual way. I have found that when this is the case, it could be that an unclean spirit has come into the person's life through the sufferings he or she has been through. This indicates that the kind of ministry to be offered is not an ordinary prayer for healing but a casting out of the spirit feeding on the sexual abuse and causing the emotional bondage. Prayer should follow, asking that the now-cleansed emotional wound be healed and inviting the Holy Spirit to occupy the ground now available to him. Wisdom is needed before a spirit is cast out. It is always good to check one's conclusions with another mature Christian before proceeding with the deliverance prayer.

Persistent Sin

Behind the whole realm of sin lies the evil one who seeks continually to capitalize on our fallen nature. When we persist in sinful habits, sexual or otherwise, we invite our spiritual enemy to tighten his grip on us. Jesus impressed upon his hearers the need to take radical measures, if necessary, to stay free from demonic bondage: "If your right eye causes you to sin, gouge it out and throw it away. It is better for you to lose one part of your body than for your whole body to be thrown into hell" (Mt 5:29).

The writer to the Hebrews warns of the danger of being hardened by the deceitful glamour of sin (Heb 3:13). The effect of this is inevitably to turn away from the living God and be caught in a web of evil. James writes that this is the beginning of a slide into spiritual death itself (Jas 1:14-15). John says that the person who abstains from persistent sinning cannot be harmed by the evil one (1 Jn 5:18). The word used here for "harm" is *haptomai* and means "fasten to or cling to." If we become careless and continually yield to the power of sin, we give our enemy freedom to fasten on to us.

All these passages imply that those who persistently sin come increasingly under the influence of the demonic. We must therefore be careful about what we look at and dwell on. It is not just repentance that is needed, although deliverance always starts there; there must also be release from evil spirits who try to build their own strongholds on the foundation of our sins.

Shock

Sometimes we are overtaken and overwhelmed by traumatic events.

At a conference on healing, I spoke with a schoolteacher who shared his deep fear of dying. He was in his early forties and, as far as he knew, he suffered from no terminal illness. None of his family had had such illnesses. The fear seemed to have come from nowhere.

As we continued to talk I noticed that he had a very slight stammer. When I asked him about this, he told me that when he was four years old he had been knocked down by a semitrailer. His first memory after the accident was of lying face up, underneath the truck, staring at its wheels. He felt terribly afraid and wondered if he had died. His stammer had emerged soon after that, and he had learned to control it only by concentrated effort. He found that he could not control it in times of pressure, when he would irrationally feel that he was going to die. His Christian faith was in constant difficulties, and he felt depressed at never seeming to "make it" in his Christian walk.

He had asked for healing from this fear on a number of occasions, but nothing had happened.

It was then that we agreed that the power behind his fear was, in fact, a spirit which had used the accident to gain access to his life. A simple prayer of authority, commanding the spirit to be cast out of his life, was enough to release him from the persistent thoughts and feelings of death. His stammer virtually disappeared and did not return even in times of pressure.

Repressed Grief

Another way in which the demonic can get a foothold is through failure to permit proper grieving after bereavement. Sometimes the bereaved person refuses to let go of a deceased relative or friend in the shock of separation.

One woman who came for counseling said she was always depressed, breaking down into extended bouts of crying for no apparent reason. Her adoptive parents had died some years before. She had never felt loved, and no matter how hard she tried she had never received warmth from her mother. When her mother died, the woman felt that there was now no further chance of persuading her mother to love her. At one level, she held on to her mother, always hoping for her love.

This is precisely where the devil can come in and seek to fulfill someone's hurt wishes. Healing came about only when the woman openly repented before the Lord and then verbally renounced her hold on her deceased mother. I commanded the evil spirit attaching her to her dead mother to come out of her.[9] She felt the heaviness leaving her. She was freed to go and live more fully and responsibly from that time.

Mourning is a valuable, necessary process. It is in acknowledging the fact of a loved one's death that we come to terms with the situation and are free to get on with our own lives.

Attack and Victory

We need to recognize, then, that there are channels through which our spiritual enemy seeks to acquire a hold on people. In this chapter, we have considered indirect routes, while involvement in the occult is a direct route. Very often, indirect enemy action can give rise to an interest in the occult: people who feel crushed and rejected by the family sometimes look to occult experiences to meet their needs for power, importance, comfort or a sense of belonging that lie unmet within them.

Through Jesus Christ, however, we have the victory over Satan and, by living in the light of God's Word, we can stand firm in the freedom for which Christ has set us free (Gal 5:1). The next chapter explores the nature of deliverance and the weapons God has provided that enable us to gain the victory in the spiritual battle.

9

Christian Deliverance Ministry

Jesus was an exorcist! He dealt with evil by his power and authority. Jesus taught that his ministry of deliverance pointed to the conquest of the kingdom of God over the kingdom of darkness. "If I drive out demons by the finger of God, then the kingdom of God has come to you" (Lk 11:20; see also Mt 12:28). Jesus was not, however, preoccupied with demonic spirits. This is a good pattern for those involved in Christian ministry. Such over-concern is unhealthy and distorts our perspective. We must follow the example of our Lord and master, aware of the dangers of our enemy, without becoming spiritual bounty hunters. Like Jesus, we should deal with evil spirits whenever they confront us; we should not go out of our way to confront them.

Our real struggle is against sin. We are not called to do battle as individuals with Satan himself. As Charles Sherlock puts it:

> The nature of our struggle follows the pattern set by Christ. His conflict with demonic (and human) opponents focussed on right rather than mere might. It centred in the cross where he took the attack of evil upon himself for our sakes, yet without violence. Thus the overcoming of Satan is closely linked with justification.[1]

Exorcism

The 1549 edition of the *Book of Common Prayer* includes the rite of exorcism. When it was revised in 1662, this rite was removed. Exorcism returned to public and church interest in 1970 when the Bishop of Exeter published his joint consultation report *Exorcism*. One of its recommendations (endorsed by Donald Coggan, then archbishop of Canterbury) was that every Anglican diocese should appoint a bishop's adviser on exorcism. This has been done in most dioceses today. This significant step recognizes the need for this kind of ministry in an increasingly pressurized world where alternative spiritual pursuits are attracting wide interest and media coverage.

There was a time when this subject was either glossed over or never mentioned in the training of ministers. I trained for three years at an evangelical Bible college, but never was I instructed about exorcism. The picture is beginning to change, however, and that is a good thing. It is better to be aware of Satan's devices than to treat the subject as so much foolishness.

The new awareness is partly due to the ministries of such people as Derek Prince and John Wimber, both of whom have taught on this subject at Christian colleges and universities in the United States. We are also recognizing the growing appeal of the occult and so-called alternative spiritual experiences, a fascination requiring a Christian response.

Be Wise

When confronted by someone in need of deliverance, then, it is wise to share your experience with a pastor rather than proceed alone. It is important to introduce your friend to those who can minister deliverance, should that be appropriate. Caution is always wise because Satan would like nothing better than our rushing in without proper preparation. This ministry is not for the novice or the person immature in the faith.

Remember the experience of the seven sons of Sceva, a Jewish chief priest, mentioned in Acts 19:13-16. They were obsessed with deliverance ministry. They thought that with a few formulas and styles of ministry they could easily proceed with this work. They tried to invoke the name of the Lord Jesus and failed. In fact, they were badly attacked by the man who was troubled by an evil spirit.

Rules and procedures are certainly not enough for taking on this ministry. To seek out occasions for deliverance is an obvious sign of immaturity. Much damage has been done by people who have read a book on this subject and felt themselves equipped to work in this area.

Further signs of immaturity are unwillingness to consult others before taking action and hastiness in drawing conclusions. Some time ago, some Christians asked me to help a woman who they said was demon-possessed. I agreed to talk with her.

The troubled woman was very nervous, and she asked me not to mention the blood of Christ or else she would faint. I assured her that it was not God's intention that she should faint and that, by working together, we might open doors for the Lord to bring in his healing and help. I listened to the story of how her marriage deeply depressed and upset her. Then I asked her why she thought she was possessed. She replied that her husband had told her so; he thought she should be free of her depressions. Because she was not, he told her that they must be due to demonic spirits. She was very angry because her husband had not listened to her and had made sweeping assumptions about her problem.

I told her that, by the grace of God, she could make a choice: to go on believing she was possessed or to face up to her own feelings and, with counsel, learn to manage them. Relieved, she chose to confront her feelings and work through them to greater healing.

This incident makes it clear that helpers must patiently listen and prayerfully discern where the real problem lies.

The Weapons of Our Warfare
Before turning to deliverance ministry, let us remind ourselves of some of our spiritual weapons.

In 2 Corinthians 10:3-5 Paul writes that Christians are fighting no ordinary war. Christian weapons have divine power to demolish strongholds. Paul was writing about arguments, pretensions and wayward thinking being overcome and demolished by the gospel in action.

Deliverance ministry overcomes strongholds in people by the power of Jesus at work in Christian ministry. It thus brings about a change in thinking and acting as people respond to Christ's lordship. Our weapons include Jesus' authority, the Word of God, the righteousness of Christ, spiritual gifts and prayer.

The Authority of Jesus
On at least three occasions Jesus sent out disciples to proclaim

the good news and to deal with spiritual need.[2] Each time, Jesus reminded them that all power and authority were his and that he would be with them. They went out, and the impact of their ministry is on record. They reported to Jesus that even the demons were subject to his name. Christians today are to work in the knowledge that at the name of Jesus every knee shall bow (Phil 2:10-11). This does not mean using the name of Jesus as a talisman; the authority of Jesus comes to every committed Christian who lives the new life of Jesus by the power of the Holy Spirit. To act in his authority is to work in cooperation with Jesus as Lord and to be channels of his power.

It is good to remind ourselves that the work of deliverance is not achieved by our techniques or our knowledge but by the authority and power of Jesus Christ.

Some years ago I was part of an evangelistic team that was visiting pubs to give out gospel leaflets and to talk about the love of Jesus with anyone who would listen. One night I went into a pub and found only two customers with the barman. One of them noticed that I was carrying a Bible. He said he knew the Bible better than I and that, because of his innumerable spiritual experiences of astral travel, there was nothing I could tell him about God. He was quite sober, sounded very sure of himself and spoke at the top of his voice.

Not to be intimidated, I found Philippians 2, which speaks of the name of Jesus being above every other name. I told him that, whatever his spiritual experience, he must submit it all to the supreme authority of Jesus Christ—whether willingly now or at the day of judgment when all secrets will be revealed. He immediately backed away from me, saying he was sorry for what he had done and that it was probably too late to change. I encouraged him to turn to Christ and open his heart to him.

He hurried out of the pub, saying he might think about it. I was amazed that his confidence in his spiritual experiences was so quickly shattered at the mention of the name of Jesus. Even though this man was unwilling to become a Christian, he recognized the superior authority of Jesus Christ.

Such incidents remind us that the authority for deliverance comes exclusively from Jesus Christ. Even the spirits recognize his authority. In Mark 1:24 and 5:7, for example, demons feared they would be judged. Those called to deliver others from demonic influence can have absolute confidence in the authority of Jesus, the source of their power.

The Word of God

Paul described scriptural truth as the "sword of the Spirit," with which Christians are helped to defeat the devil (Eph 6:16-17). Jesus himself knew this, and he used Scripture to rebuff the temptations he endured in the wilderness. His replies began with the words, "It is written." The Word of God is an offensive weapon for times of spiritual warfare. When helping people who are in bondage to evil, we often need to reassure them of God's promises of forgiveness and cleansing. Jesus said that only truth will set captives free; the devil is a liar (Jn 8:36, 44).

Once, after I had been involved in a major deliverance ministry, I was called out again by the husband of the woman who had received ministry. He said that his wife was showing signs of stress, and he asked me for another deliverance session. I was a little alarmed, for I felt that the necessary work had been done.

It turned out that what the woman needed was reassurance from the Bible that her sins really had been forgiven. She had begun to think that since she did not deserve God's love and healing, he might not really have accepted her. I shared some Bible verses with her, underscoring that, if we confess our sins, God is "faithful and just and will forgive us our sins and purify us from all unrighteousness" (1 Jn 1:9).

The Bible assures us of God's faithfulness and justice; this she could hold on to. It proved a solid foundation for the rebuilding of her life and renewing of her faith.

After people have received healing through deliverance, they need nurturing in their newfound freedom. The Scriptures are our prime resource for this.

The Righteousness of Christ

When Paul describes the hardships of the Christian life, he also refers to our resources for strength and conquest. Among these are "the weapons of righteousness" (2 Cor 6:7). It is our righteousness before God through Jesus Christ that gives us confidence to exercise the authority and power of Jesus.

Of course we are sinners, and we still fall. But we should stand boldly on the truth that we have been given the righteousness of Christ. God, by forgiving us and saving us, has placed us in his Son Jesus Christ. Being in right standing with God, we can go forward to serve him with confidence. I have always found it useful, before praying with someone for deliverance, to confess my own need of Jesus' love and forgiveness and to thank him for giving me these gifts.

Spiritual Gifts

The gifts of the Spirit are not optional extras for the Christian. On a number of occasions we are encouraged to seek earnestly the gifts that will aid our growth and work (1 Cor 12:1, 31; 14:1, 39). I do not believe, however, that deliverance ministry is the prerogative solely of charismatic or Pentecostal Christians.

One of the gifts mentioned in 1 Corinthians 12 is "discernment of spirits." This is vital in the work of healing. We need to know God's guidance on the source of particular phenomena—is it the person's own sick mind, some outside influence or emotional control, or a demonic spirit? If it is a spirit, what aspect of the person's life is being affected? The answers to these questions enable us to focus our prayer and ministry more sharply. We may need to know whether to command a spirit to cease troubling someone physically or whether to set someone's emotional hurts free from demonic influence. There may also be a need to ask the Holy Spirit to bring light and freedom to a person's mind because he or she has been led astray by false doctrines and wrong behavior. When Jesus was explaining why the disciples could not help the boy in Mark 9, he said, "This kind can come out only by prayer." Sometimes, deliverance prayer may be ineffective because we have not appreciated what kind of spirit is at work. To take Jesus' advice, we need to pray before ministry in order to prepare ourselves properly for the work in hand.

It is not within the scope of this book to explain the nature of the spiritual gifts, but here are two examples of spiritual gifts.

One minister, just as he was sitting down to dinner, found the mother of a distressed child on his doorstep, pleading with him to come with her right away. As he went to her house he quietly and desperately prayed that the Lord would show him what to do. When he stood before the upset girl, he felt that God had given a spiritual gift of faith, which gave him confidence that his prayers would be answered. His faith had been strengthened for the work of deliverance that was now needed. Quite calmly, he commanded the girl to be delivered from any spirit that was tormenting her. Although she initially resisted, he repeated that the spirit must get out and not bother the girl or anyone else again. The girl then experienced great release and felt calm again. Later, both mother and daughter repented of having consulted a gypsy medium. They embraced Jesus as Savior. Since then they have been growing steadily in the Christian faith.

Some years ago I was asked to pray for a woman and her baby, who seemed not to be growing properly. Although a year old, the baby did not move around. In addition, the mother had been having nightmares and felt oppressed by voices in her mind. I asked the Lord to show me what to do. It seemed very hard to pray at the time, and I could not get my thoughts together.

The thought suddenly came to me that the woman had been lying and that she had been poisoning her baby. I decided to mention this.

The mother confessed that she felt very depressed at times and hated her daughter. Consequently she had begun to give her drugs. She was truly sorry for her actions and asked God to forgive her. She also mentioned that she was living with another man and that her husband had begun divorce proceedings. All of this made her feel increasingly resentful until she seemed full of hatred. After prayer for freedom from this hatred, she was able to manage her feelings more successfully. The baby recovered from the effects of the drugs and was later found to be perfectly normal.

I would encourage all Christians who engage in deliverance ministry to stay open to the Holy Spirit so that in time of need they may receive a gift from God to help them in their work.

Prayer

Prayer is, of course, the foundation of all ministry. We must spend time with God in order to know him better and to be sensitive to the ways in which he guides our work. When Paul listed the pieces of a Christian's battle armor, the climactic piece is prayer: "Pray in the Spirit on all occasions with all kinds of prayers and requests" (Eph 6:18).

We can never overemphasize the need for prayer. Jesus repeatedly went aside to pray. John 17 even tells us that three times he went aside to pray the same prayer. Interestingly, he concentrated on asking for strength and unity among his disciples. The dark hour was coming and it was vitally important that the disciples should not abandon their faith. Jesus prayed earnestly both for them and for himself. And in the Garden of Gethsemane, before his greatest conflict with evil, he prayed.

It is in prayer that we draw near to God and he draws near to us. Prayer is how we get our roots down into the spiritual life of God himself. In prayer, we learn to listen to his voice.

If we are to exercise authority in ministry, it will be by making prayer a priority. When Moses came down from the mountain, having spent time with God, his face shone with the wonder of that fellowship. In a similar way, the Christian, having spent time with the Lord in prayer, is to radiate his presence.

These, then, are some of our weapons. They should be spiritual disciplines for all Christians—we are all, to varying degrees, involved in spiritual warfare. But some will be involved in a specific ministry to those who need a more radical kind of deliverance from enemy captivity: exorcism.

10

Praying for Deliverance

*People who need deliverance ministry are understandably anx-*ious about their condition. They need loving reassurance before ministry begins. We should avoid treating the subject in a sensational manner; the work is to be done quietly and with plenty of individual care. The problem is not to be treated as the *big* sin, so that people are made to feel inferior or worse sinners than those who suffer from so-called lesser illnesses—or none at all.

We should always remember that this work is only a part of the overall healing ministry of Jesus. Our goal is not just to break bondages but to bring healing. All the Gospel writers include spiritual oppression when they list various sicknesses. Mark, for example, says, "the people brought to Jesus all the sick and demon-possessed . . . and Jesus healed many who had various diseases. He also drove out many demons" (Mk 1:32, 34). Matthew, writing of the same events, uses the term *healing* to include deliverance itself (Mt 4:24; 8:16-17). These verses should encourage us to remember that the purpose of this work is to bring healing and wholeness.

Spiritual bondage is simply one category of disease, while deliverance and exorcism can be classed together as one kind of healing. This could explain why the list of spiritual gifts in 1 Corinthians 12 includes healing, discernment and miraculous powers—but not exorcism.

Working Together
In this chapter we shall consider some common "symptoms" of demonic captivity. Then we will look at five steps in the process of bringing deliverance to those in spiritual bondage.

Let me re-emphasize that when we get involved with deliverance ministry it is well to seek advice and, whenever possible, to work alongside a fellow Christian for mutual support. We should never rush into this ministry or give way to the temptation to react on the spur of the moment. It is sound practice to consult one's pastor or another spiritual counselor before proceeding.

No matter how experienced we may be, we should not try to be lone rangers operating outside pastoral and church support. Such people tend to become a law unto themselves, and this independence will not encourage those they help to join a local church. Even Paul and Barnabas reported to their church leadership on the various ministries they were engaged in.

Identifying the Need
We have already underlined the need for careful interviewing

before deliverance prayer. Michael Green suggests that if more troubled people really experienced forgiveness, and forgave others, then the number of exorcisms might be halved.[1] If counseling and repentance with prayer seem to suffice, we need not proceed to confront the demonic. Leon Suenens adds this cautionary word:

> No demon of lust was expelled from the adulterous woman (John 8), or from the woman of ill-repute mentioned by Luke (chapter 7), or from the incestuous people of Corinth (1 Corinthians 5). No demon of avarice was expelled from Zacchaeus, no demon of incredulity from Peter after his triple betrayal. No demon of rivalry was expelled from the Corinthians whom Paul had to call to order.[2]

Counselors must ask themselves whether simple repentance and prayer or full exorcism is needed. Exorcism, as we have said, is less common, and it is usually characterized by a degree of uncontrollable behavior. People needing exorcism usually experience greater distress.

Recognizing the Need for Exorcism

John Richards, in his book *But Deliver Us from Evil,* gives a very helpful list of symptoms by which to recognize those who are suffering from acute demonic attack and in need of exorcism.

Change of Personality

Under the acute attack of the enemy, a person may experience changes in intelligence, moral character, demeanor and appearance. Some years ago I was approached by a young man whose sister had undergone dramatic personality changes as a result of attending a religious festival in which the participants were encouraged to invite the spirits to come and possess them. His sister was normally quiet and kindly, but she had rapidly become aggressive, angry and continuously drunken. Only exorcism brought about a return to her usual behavior.

Physical Changes

Physical changes in the person may include the following:

1. Unnatural strength, as in the man named Legion, who could break the chains that bound him (Mk 5:4).

2. Convulsions; foaming at the mouth (Lk 9:39).

3. Catatonic symptoms; falling. The man called Legion is said to have fallen down on his knees in front of Jesus. The context shows that this was not an act of worship (Mk 5:6). Compare this example with those found in Matthew 17:15 (the "epileptic" boy) and Luke 4:35 (the man in the synagogue).

4. Clouding of consciousness; insensitivity to pain.

5. Changed voice. Those engaged in exorcism sometimes report that another voice (often of the opposite sex) speaks through the person being delivered. Jesus is certainly addressed by possessing spirits, as all of the above-mentioned accounts testify. However—a cautionary note—Jesus did not engage in conversation with the spirits but commanded them to shut up and come out.

Mental Changes

1. Ability to speak or understand unknown languages. Many of those involved in spiritism or other cultic groups report that they can "speak in tongues." This should not surprise us when we remember how much the Bible refers to false gods and pseudo-spirituality. It is an attempt at counterfeiting the real.

2. Preternatural knowledge. Those who have a possessing

spirit seem to have accurate knowledge of things, ranging from personal information on the one who has come to offer exorcism to events in everyday life. This is true of those who practice fortunetelling and astrology. Interestingly, the Bible does not warn so much about false prophecy as about false prophets. The test is whether the person lives to the glory of God and his Son Jesus Christ and whether his or her life conforms to the biblical pattern. We must recognize that demonic spirits do have a certain amount of knowledge of things largely hidden to human beings. In the Bible, possessing spirits often knew who Jesus was and instantly recognized his power over them.

3. Psychic and occultic powers.

Spiritual Changes

Spiritual changes are likely to be evident in those under acute attack.

1. Reaction to and fear of Christ. This fear is not usually expressed, however, unless ministry of some kind is being offered.

2. Reaction to prayer. As above, there can be a kind of apathy until prayer with authority is offered. I remember praying with a woman who came for counseling because she felt there was something within her that seemed to have a life of its own. She was obviously distressed but was able to talk about her situation with some control. When I began to pray, however, she twisted and turned. Then she said, "It hurts, please stop." After some discussion I soon realized that it was an evil spirit within her that was reacting to the prayer. But with the woman's permission and cooperation, we proceeded with an exorcism which saw her delivered and brought to faith in Jesus Christ.

Praying for Deliverance

People suffering acute demonic influence need exorcism. This must be conducted by those who are qualified for the task, never by a novice in the faith. No one should tackle it alone. Fortunately, most of the people I have counseled didn't need a full-scale exorcism.

We shall now examine the process of praying for deliverance, the most common need of those bothered by spirits. The form which I shall be outlining is not a technique or a foolproof formula. It is one suggested procedure among many for effecting deliverance. We should always remember that the work is the Lord's and the power is the Lord's. Our part is to obey him and to be faithful to him and his church.

The five steps to take in praying for deliverance are: recognition of the problem, repentance, renunciation of evil, release from the evil spirit's bondage and renewal of spiritual life.

Recognition

Prayerfully examine the individual's problem; never assume it is demonic. Get as much detailed information as you can about the person's experience, symptoms, and recent family history. Make a note of any occasions when shock or emotional damage occurred. If the person has been seeing a doctor, ask permission to talk to the doctor.

Ask if the person has received prayer counseling before. If so, what form did it take, and were there any benefits? Ask if there has been any involvement in the occult by the individual or any member of the family. (See the appendix for an example of this kind of questioning.) If after covering all this you are still convinced that an evil spirit is at work, it is time to take a step of faith and openly acknowledge your conviction before God.

Very often, the one in need is not only bound but passive. Those coming for help must not be allowed to think that the counselor can do all the work alone, while they sit back and receive. It will not do for them to be spectators in the proceedings. Their own faith must be activated so that they get involved in their own deliverance. This includes not only being willing to be set free, but being totally honest about their condition.

We must avoid playing deliverance games. In the anxiety to be healed and set free, people can be tempted to agree with whatever is said by those who are doing the ministry. They can come to regard deliverance as the cure for all ills. Deliverance must not be seen as an easy alternative to the hard work of counseling to get to the root of the problem.

When it's clear that there is spiritual bondage, the person must openly admit a need for deliverance and then ask for it. This is not as easy as it sounds, especially for Christians. They can be reluctant to admit that they've let their spiritual enemy gain a foothold. Some Christians, rather than admit that they have such a problem, have simply let their faith decline.

Once I was leading a church's weekend conference and felt guided to speak on spiritual victory. I gave some time to explaining that Christians can sometimes need deliverance in the name of Jesus. My text was that part of the Lord's Prayer which says, "But deliver us from evil." This, I said, was no paper tiger of a prayer. Jesus, by giving it as a pattern prayer, was implying that from time to time and in various ways, Christians would need deliverance from evil.

When I ended my talk, having outlined some of the symptoms of demonic influence, I gave an invitation for prayer. At first there was silence. Then, about seventeen people asked for prayer, outlining the areas of their lives in which they felt bound. Included in the seventeen was a married couple who faithfully served their local fellowship. Despite prayer for inner healing and forgiveness, they had struggled for years with feelings of resentment and anger toward each other. The husband, particularly, said he had found it hard to admit he needed deliverance; he was afraid of losing his wife's respect. Both received deliverance prayer, and both said they suddenly felt free from the destructive aggression which had dogged their married life. Now, years later, they are still free from their bondage and have gone on to grow in the power of the Spirit and to develop ministries of their own together. Their transformation began when they confessed their need, recognized their problem and took an active part in their own deliverance.

Another way in which people can be encouraged to recognize their need and to be actively involved is to ask them for their own impressions from time to time. It does not hinder the work of deliverance if the helper occasionally asks how the other person is feeling. This prevents the helper from running blindly ahead and keeps everyone in touch with what is happening.

Repentance

After recognizing their need, people seeking deliverance must turn from sin and look to God. This is repentance. It is always good to invite people to say their own prayer of repentance aloud. James tells us to confess our sins to one another and pray for one another so that we may be healed (Jas 5:16).

I have always enjoyed learning spiritual truths through the children's stories in Paul White's *Jungle Doctor* books (published by Paternoster Press). One in particular comes to mind in connection with repentance.

White describes the African way to catch a monkey. First you make a hole in a coconut, just big enough to allow a monkey to insert his hand. You fill the coconut with smaller nuts and fix it firmly to the ground with a stake. Then sit out of sight and wait for the monkey to come in search of food. The monkey will slip his hand into the coconut and grab a fistful of nuts. But he cannot pull his hand out of the hole—because it is full of nuts! All the monkey has to do to be free again is to let go of the nuts. But he won't. And that is how a trapper can catch a monkey.

This story aptly describes the relationship between repentance and freedom. If our hands are full of the "nuts" of our sinful living, and we are not willing to let go of them in repentance, we are in no position to receive the forgiveness of God. We are still trapped in our sins. Basilea Schlink highlights this connection between repentance and freedom when she says that it is as we repent that the kingdom of God draws near to us, and this leads to the joy of living freely in the Father's presence.[3] Repentance opens us up to the forgiveness and power of God. Similarly, we also need to forgive others.

One Palm Sunday, an anxious mother phoned me. Her married daughter was in some distress and speaking with a strange voice. Would I come? Fortunately a member of our lay-ministry team was also available, and, after a time of prayer, we went to the house to meet the daughter.

She was very pale, curled up tightly on a sofa and moaning. Before we commenced any prayer for deliverance we invited her to turn to God, and she did read out a prayer which I carried inside my Bible. Here is that prayer, which I have encouraged others to use from time to time:

Lord Jesus Christ, I believe you died on the cross for my sins and rose again from the dead. You redeemed me by your

blood and I belong to you, and I want to live for you. I
confess all my sins—known and unknown—I'm sorry for
them all. I renounce them all. I forgive all others as I want
you to forgive me. Forgive me now and cleanse me with your
blood. I thank you for the blood of Jesus Christ which
cleanses me from all sin. And I come to you now as my
deliverer. You know my special needs—the thing that binds,
that torments, that defiles: that evil spirit, that unclean spirit—I claim the promise of your word, "Whosoever calleth on
the name of the Lord will be saved." I call upon you now.
In the name of the Lord Jesus Christ, deliver me and set me
free. Satan, I renounce you and all your works. I loose myself
from you in the name of Jesus, and I command you to leave
me right now, in Jesus's name! Amen.[4]

During the deliverance ministry that followed, difficult as it was
at times, it was encouraging to know that the girl was working
with us for her own healing. Whenever I asked her if she was
managing to keep her faith centered on Jesus Christ, she would
respond slowly and deliberately in the words of the baptismal
liturgy: "I believe and trust in him." It was repentance that
turned her toward Jesus as Savior. She called on the Lord even
as she was being freed from the bondage of evil spirits.

Renunciation

In order to be free, we must speak out against the bondage we
experience and give it over to God. Those involved in the occult
in Ephesus gave up all their books on magic as a way of renouncing evil and embracing the gospel (Acts 19:18-20). Anything connected with the occult should be destroyed or surrendered. This removes any remaining link with former occult
practices; it is a way of burning bridges.

I once ministered to a young man who had been experimenting with various forms of black magic. He was feeling more and more afraid, and he came to ask for prayer. He wanted to receive peace and to be freed of his growing apprehension and fear. Even when he received prayer, however, his condition did not change. It was only when he renounced his involvement with black magic and got rid of all the objects he had used in worship that he began to respond to prayer and was eventually set free completely.

Renouncing also helps people to confront any fear they may have about being freed and healed. Deliverance can often be a struggle and a painful process, and much love and care must be exercised. We must not push people into renunciation but, rather, invite them to do so, so that it is their genuine choice.

Such renunciation may also deal with any hidden resentments that may come suddenly to the fore. Once, when I was encouraging someone to renounce his involvement with the occult, he said quite loudly, "I can't do it!" So I stopped the prayer time and invited him to talk about it. Doubts came to light: "What if it doesn't work? Will I be attacked again?" It is always healthier to talk about such fears than to suppress them with an exhortation to get on with it and trust the Lord. It is perfect love that casts out fear, not hurried quotations from the Bible or noisy encouragements to go forward. We sometimes need to take time to affirm the love of God and to examine the fear, so that we know where to direct this love in prayer.

Sometimes the act of renunciation can take a question-and-answer form. The responses give an opportunity to reject any evil which has been part of a person's life. The form can be similar to the Anglican baptismal liturgy in which the candidate is asked, "Do you turn to Christ?" and replies, "I turn to Christ." The following act of renunciation is offered as a suggested structure. Remember, though, that it is faith in action which is the key—not a set formula.

Do you renounce the devil and those powers which rebel against God?
I do.
Do you renounce all your sinful desires which have drawn you away from the love of Jesus Christ?
I do.
Do you renounce [mention any specific occult practice in which he or she may have been involved]?
I do.

Release

Once the person has specifically renounced evil, we can take the offensive. Now is the time for the prayer of command by which the hold of the evil spirit is broken and the person is set free from its influence.

The verb used over thirty times in the New Testament in the context of deliverance is *ekballo,* translated as "drive out" in the New International Version. The word literally means "throw out with force and purpose." It implies direct confrontation and even violence. John Richards likes to translate it "chuck out," as this implies getting rid of material that we do not want and are glad to get rid of.

Many of Jesus' words of deliverance are remarkably short. They take the form of commands such as "Go" and "Be quiet! . . . Come out of him!" (Mt 8:32; Mk 1:25). This should remind us that there is no need for long sessions of prayer for those seeking deliverance. Jesus spoke in the authority he had as the

Son of God. We in our praying must stand on that same authority of Christ.

It is best to keep the prayers simple. Where possible, use prayers familiar to the people undergoing deliverance or encourage them to pray their own brief prayer.

Most Christians know the Lord's Prayer, and it is good to invite the individual to join you in saying it. It begins with the exaltation of God and then moves on to human needs, which include sustenance ("Give us this day our daily bread"), guidance ("Lead us not into temptation"), renunciation ("But deliver us from the evil one") and praise to God ("For thine is the kingdom, and the power and the glory"). A simple prayer of deliverance may follow. Here is one example:

Lord God of hosts, before your presence the armies of hell are put to flight. Deliver [name] from the assaults and temptations of the evil one. Free [him/her] from every evil and unclean spirit that may be assailing [him/her]. Strengthen and protect [name] by the power of your Holy Spirit, through Jesus Christ our Lord. Amen.[5]

We rebuke the evil one now and command in the name of Jesus Christ that you do not trouble [name] anymore. In the name of Jesus, get out and do not trouble [him/her] anymore.

As we identify the nature or names of the evil spirits present, it may be necessary to address them more specifically and directly. Jesus addressed deaf and mute or unclean spirits before casting them out. He identified or located the principle area in which an evil spirit troubled a person. We may suppose that he received this knowledge by the gift of discernment. This enabled him to know that some people's physical disabilities (such as muteness) were not physical but spiritual in origin.

When I prayed with someone once, it became apparent that he was in the grip of a spirit of fear. This was a conviction brought about by the guidance of the Holy Spirit. The fear in question was not responding to any of the conventional means of counsel and care. I felt that the Holy Spirit was encouraging me to recognize a spiritual basis for the fear. Our prayer went something like this: "We bind you, spirit of fear, in the name of Jesus, and command you to get out of [name]'s life right now. Go, in the name of Jesus, and do not trouble [name] anymore. Amen."

This command may have to be repeated once or twice with authority before complete release is achieved. We are not bargaining with our enemy; we are evicting him as the trespasser that he is. Therefore, we issue a command.

The Deliverance Prayer

The deliverance prayer, then, should include the following elements: binding the spirit, commanding the spirit to go and forbidding the spirit to return or to do further harm.

Binding the spirit. Jesus said that he cast out demons "by the Spirit of God" (Mt 12:28). (This again reminds us of the real source of our power to minister in the name of Jesus.) He went on to give a picture of deliverance in action: "How can anyone enter a strong man's house and carry off his possessions unless he first ties up [binds] the strong man?" (Mt 12:29).

It is clear that deliverance involves limiting the influence of the spirit which is bothering the individual. When I was praying with a man for deliverance from a violent spirit, he interrupted me with a challenge. He said that the voices inside him were laughing and saying that they were not going to leave him alone. I stopped praying and took Jesus' words to heart. I addressed these "voices" and said that in the name of Jesus they had no power—from now on they were to shut up, as I was binding them so that they could no longer intimidate the man. He responded that they had gone silent and that this reassured him of the authority of Christ to heal him—which subsequently happened.

There are a number of ways of binding spirits. Jesus, we have read, commanded them to be silent. At times it will be appropriate to remind such spirits of the victory and majesty of God through quoting the words of Scripture. This Jesus did in the face of his own testing in the wilderness.

Some years ago, a friend and I were praying with a man for deliverance. It was in danger of going on far too long, and we felt weak and tired. Then my friend began to extol the glorious wonders of the love of God and the greatness of his Son Jesus Christ. It seemed to release new energy into us, and the person we were seeking to help said he felt his anxiety diminish. He became aware of an inner release from troubles that had bothered him for almost twenty years.

The writer to the Hebrews also spoke of binding or limiting the influence of spirits. "Since the children have flesh and blood, he too shared in their humanity so that by his death he might destroy him who holds the power of death—that is, the devil—and free those who all their lives were held in slavery by their fear of death."[6]

The word for "destroy" used here is *katargeo,* which can be translated "render powerless" or "reduce to inactivity." Jesus exercised binding in his ministry, and, because of Jesus' death and resurrection, the Christian can do likewise.

Commanding the spirit to go. We have already emphasized that the Christian has the authority of Jesus Christ to minister in his name. We should remember that when the disciples were first commissioned to proclaim the good news of the kingdom of God, they were given both power and authority to do this (Lk 9:1). This directive is repeated in the Great Commission, which shows such ministry being passed on to all disciples of Jesus, as new Christians are taught to obey all that Jesus commanded and in their turn teach others. Deliverance ministry implies conflict with evil, and we therefore need dynamic power from God and the confidence to exercise that power. That is authority.

Should the demon resist the command to depart (and this is certainly not uncommon), we will need to stand on the fact that God has given us his power if we are to persevere in faith until the spirit has been removed. The fact that we can, by the grace of God, command evil spirits to go in this way reminds us that the kingdom of God is coming in, breaking people's bondage to evil. This is the essence of the gospel itself: Jesus has come to set us free to love and serve him in newness of life. Donald Bridge goes so far as to say that there can be no real and relevant proclamation of the gospel without a confrontation with Satan, for "the god of this age has blinded the minds of unbelievers, so that they cannot see the light of the gospel."[7]

Bridge goes on to refer to the statement of the Lausanne Committee on World Evangelization that signs should accompany evangelism by the church; one sign, the third sign of the kingdom of God, is exorcism. John Wimber speaks of the three great marks of the kingdom as being evangelism, healing and exorcism.[8]

Such divisions are at least a little artificial. Our evangelists should not expect deliverance to occur every time they proclaim the gospel. They should be forewarned about evil spirits in order to be able to deal with them when occasion demands; yet it is better to put the emphasis on the nature of sin and our need to see people soundly converted and growing in discipleship.

When we encounter the demonic, it is to be dealt with. We should then move on to the greater work of encouraging holiness of life. After all, according to the Scriptures, the chief goal of Satan is not to possess people but to keep them from knowing the glory of Christ. Christian ministry should therefore encourage people to enter into the new life of Jesus and be changed from one degree of glory to another. This, perhaps, is the greatest evidence of the defeat of Satan.

Let us not be afraid, then, to be militant when it comes to deliverance prayer. After all, we do not address the troubled person, but the spirit, which is an enemy. Paul describes our conflict as warfare, and we should conduct ourselves as disciplined fighting troops.

Bridge mentions that some revisers of the *Methodist Hymn Book* have expressed discomfort with the military metaphors of some hymns. While I would not want to glorify warfare, I think such a reaction is misplaced. The early disciples certainly took the offensive against evil, with remarkable results. The evangelical revival out of which the Methodist church developed certainly witnessed great conflicts with evil and many triumphs through the power of Christ. No wonder Charles Wesley wrote such stirring lines as:

Jesus, the name high over all
    In hell, or earth, or sky!
Angels and men before it fall
And devils fear and fly.

From every evil motion freed
(The Son hath made us free),
On all the powers of hell we tread
In glorious liberty.

Forbidding the spirit to return. In the account of the boy who was delivered from a spirit that had plagued him from childhood, Jesus commanded the spirit not to re-enter the boy (Mk 9:25). This implies that, once a person is delivered, the problem may recur unless preventive measures are taken. There are two ways of doing this.

The first is to command the spirit not to return. Some people have been sidetracked into discussing where the spirits actually go. This is certainly not what the Bible focuses on. We must simply cut the person off from the spirit and command the spirit never to return. It may be helpful to say something like, "In the name of Jesus, I command you never to return here and to be kept bound until the day of Christ's judgment."

The other preventive measure is to ensure that the person delivered offers to God his or her newly won freedom. We have already referred to Jesus' statement about the possibility of being delivered but ending up in a worse state than before (Mt 12:43-45). Jesus is not suggesting that our deliverance is insecure, but he is urging us to build on what God has done and make certain we are filled with the Holy Spirit.

This brings us, then, to the final element in this process of deliverance: renewal.

Renewal

The process of deliverance can be physically and emotionally tiring for the prayer team as well as for the person delivered.

It is good and practical to provide space for rest, food and drink if possible.

Once the work of deliverance has been completed and all concerned are satisfied that the presence and power of evil have been broken, the individual needs care and follow-up. This is not an optional extra but an essential element in the renewal of spiritual life and the maintenance of that freedom.

This is not the time to launch into exhaustive exhortations. After some simple prayers for protection and a good night's sleep, the helpers should arrange for one of the team, the pastor perhaps, to call back within a day or so. At that point counsel for the person's ongoing growth and freedom in Jesus can be offered.

The following are some practical ways in which we can build up someone who has experienced God's deliverance.

Fellowship. It is essential for Christians to belong to a local church which will be their spiritual home. Here they will find support and love, a proper climate in which they can mature with God.

It is a great help for those released from spiritual bondage to share in the sacraments, outward signs of the inward realities they have recently experienced. Those who have not been baptized should be encouraged to take this step of faith. It seals for them in public the inward experience of the cleansing, saving and healing power of Jesus which has delivered them. The same is true of sharing in communion.

Some years ago I took part in a fairly demanding deliverance. The pastor invited the woman who had received help to come to communion the following day. Since she had never taken communion before and was not a member of his church, she asked whether it would be right to do so. The pastor replied that the communion celebrates what the Lord Jesus has done for us; it would be entirely appropriate for her to come and join in that occasion. She did so, and later she reported that she felt the Lord encouraging her with the knowledge that she was truly a born-again member of his living body. She has since gone from strength to strength. We must make sure, then, that people delivered from spiritual bondage go on to grow in the fellowship of Christ's church.

Filling and freedom. Those parts of our lives that were under the domination of evil must be deliberately offered to God under the lordship of Jesus Christ.

People sometimes say that they feel lighter and "emptier" after deliverance. This reminds us that this newly won space must be filled with the Spirit of the living God. When someone knows from experience the domination of an evil spirit, it is good to assure him or her of the effects of being filled with the Holy Spirit. He brings us the new life of God and frees us to serve him. He has come to make the life and presence of Jesus real within us and evident through us. In his service is perfect freedom.

Discipline. Once set free, people must not fall back into the habits that brought them into bondage. If they have been engaged in some occult practice or have belonged to a religious cult, they must break all association with it. If the problem originated in drug-taking or sexual promiscuity, they must make every effort to stay free of such things. They should not "test" themselves to see if they can withstand the things which once overpowered them, as this useful parable warns us:

> Once upon a time, there was a man who lived in a castle at the top of a very steep hill. The only way to get to the house was up a narrow, winding road, at the side of which was a steep cliff.

One day the man went down into the town in order to hire a new coach-driver. Three men came to be interviewed for the job.

The man asked the first applicant, "Do you drive well enough to take me up and down to my castle in safety?"

The driver replied, "I can take you up and down to your castle and drive you within twelve inches of the edge of the cliff, and you will still be safe with me."

The owner of the castle asked the same question of the next applicant, who answered, "I can take you up and down to your castle and drive you within six inches of the edge of the cliff, and you will still be safe with me."

Finally, the third driver was asked the same question, and he replied, "I can take you up and down to your castle, but I will stay as far away from the edge of the cliff as I can, and you will be safe with me."

Which of the drivers do you think got the job? The third driver was not prepared to flirt with danger. Those who have been delivered must rigorously put into practice that part of the Lord's Prayer which says "Lead us not into temptation." It is no use praying this if we do not play our part. We must not flirt with evil. We need the disciplines of faithful reading and study of the Bible, constant prayer, and growth in love and obedience to Christ.

The armor of God offers us protection from spiritual attack (Eph 6:10-18). Paul's words on this theme challenge the Christian to be prepared for spiritual attack, equipped with truth, dependent on Christ's righteousness for our salvation, growing in faith and prayerfulness, and fighting the enemy with the Word of God.

Counsel and healing. Now that the situation can be looked

at without the complication of demonic activity, counseling may be needed to deal with emotional hurts and wounds.

One person who had received such ministry needed help to confront some underlying problems. He had a long-standing hatred of his father, who had broken up the family and remarried when his son was a little child. The new wife did not want the boy, and so he had been passed around to various members of the family. His hurt had turned to a deep-seated bitterness which gave an evil spirit a foothold. Now that he had been set free, he needed to forgive his father and let go of his hatred. As well as bringing emotional healing, this ensured that the hurt did not remain vulnerable to attack and oppression in the future.

During recovery after deliverance, we must be alert to any underlying hurts or issues which may surface and need counsel. This can be the most time-consuming part of the ministry, and the temptation is to gloss over it. This would be a big mistake.

Praise and worship. A great help in consolidating one's healing and freedom is to give thanks to God for his victory and increasingly to worship him. This attitude reflects a wholehearted devotion and commitment to Jesus Christ. God inhabits the praises of his people (Ps 22:3), and as we praise him he draws near to love and renew us.

I am reminded of the story of the fall of Jericho, told in Joshua 6. The priests with their trumpets, and the people with their festive shout of praise, toppled the walls and signaled the victory that was to follow. When we praise God we signal his victory for us and we are glad! This is a necessary resource for those who may not feel very strong and who begin to wonder if they have been freed and if they will remain so. Feelings are not always reliable, but praise reminds us of the constant truth of who God is and what he has done for us.

Follow-up is vital if the newly delivered person is to maintain freedom in Jesus and grow in the Christian faith. Above all, the person needs to be assured of the victory of Jesus and his power to keep all those who have entrusted their lives to him. A good passage to share with those who have been set free by the power of Jesus is Paul's assurance that God will never abandon them. He is determined to keep them by his love and grace.

In spite of all, overwhelming victory is ours through him who loved us. For I am convinced that there is nothing in death or life, in the realm of spirits or superhuman powers, in the world as it is or the world as it shall be, in the forces of the universe, in heights or depths—nothing in all creation that can separate us from the love of God in Christ Jesus our Lord. (Rom 8:37-39 NEB)

11

Signs of
Deliverance

When a person is set free from the power of evil, there may be some manifestations as the evil spirit is removed. This should not alarm us. Such signs accompanied the ministry of Jesus and, at times (but not always), they were quite noisy and dramatic. When Jesus delivered the boy mentioned in Mark 9, for example, the boy convulsed and fell to the ground as if dead. Other manifestations mentioned in the Bible include crying out, shaking and falling.

Crying Out and Shouting

Just then a man in their synagogue who was possessed by an evil spirit cried out, "What do you want with us?"[1]

When he [Jesus] arrived at the other side . . . two demon-possessed men coming from the tombs met him. . . . "What do you want with us, Son of God?" they shouted. (Mt 8:28-29)

Such responses indicate that the evil spirit recognizes the authority of Jesus and understands that it will soon be expelled. While we should not encourage such remarks, we should take courage from them; they are a sign that Jesus is working through us.

Shaking and Falling

The evil spirit shook the man violently. (Mk 1:26)

Whenever the evil spirits saw him, they fell down before him.[2]

"Be quiet!" Jesus said sternly. "Come out of him!" Then the demon threw the man down before them all and came out without injuring him. (Lk 4:35)

In addition to the above, other manifestations of deliverance, not specifically mentioned in the Bible and milder in form, may also be experienced: coughing, shivering, yawning and even belching might occur.

The person being delivered can sometimes be quite upset. We need to offer reassurance that the Lord is doing his work. When any manifestations take place, therefore, we must not dwell on them but press on until deliverance is complete. Remember that Jesus rarely entered into conversation with demons. He forbade the spirit to speak, he commanded it to be quiet, and he ordered it to come out. We should do likewise and not indulge in prolonged, unhelpful conversations.

Sometimes, when deliverance prayer is under way, a person may be aware of the evil spirit in a particular part of the body. We have mentioned that some spirits caused deafness and dumbness and that Jesus commanded the spirits of deafness to come out. I do not think it is stretching the biblical account to say that it is quite likely that such spirits had a hold over these physical organs and that they needed to be dislodged.

When such manifestations occur I have found it appropriate to pray for the affected parts of the body. With due sensitivity I have asked the person to place his or her hands on the affected part while I commanded the spirit to let go and never harm anyone else again. It is not essential to use the hands in this way, but it is sometimes a helpful focus for those praying as well as for the sufferer.

When I was praying with a man for deliverance after involvement with the Ouija board, he felt a tremendous pain in his back. He placed his hand on the lower part of his back, and I ordered the spirit to get off his back and not return. The man felt heat on the affected part, and, suddenly, both the pain and his spiritual bondage were gone.

What If Nothing Happens?

Sometimes there are no apparent manifestations. Does this mean the work has not been successful and needs to be repeated? Graham Powell says that in all the deliverances he has conducted, only two-thirds of the people experienced manifestations, and, for the most part, they were fairly mild.[3] There are several accounts in the New Testament of people being delivered from demons with no manifestations whatsoever.[4]

Christian ministry is primarily a work of faith. We are called to follow the principles laid down in God's Word. The writer to the Hebrews tells us that faith is being sure of what we hope for and certain of what we do not see (Heb 11:1).

So we should not be concerned if we see no immediate response to our ministry. We should encourage the individual to trust in God and his sure promises—not in manifestations or good feelings. The real evidence that the work has been done will be in the consequent freedom and development of spiritual life, especially if the one delivered takes on the disciplines and faithfulness essential to ongoing spiritual renewal.

Sometimes deliverance simply does not happen. This failure may be due to a lack of authority in those praying. Authority does not consist in a fervent pumping up of excitement and noise. On the other hand, quiet politeness will not impress the demonic powers either! Those praying for deliverance must ensure that they believe in what they are doing and that they have faith in Christ and his supreme authority to act in response to their faith.

Michael Perry points out that another cause of failure to secure freedom is an unbalanced use of time. It is best to devote most of the time to the interview stage of the ministry and less to the deliverance prayer itself. Listening will help us to determine the direction the ministry should take. If we gloss over the need for repentance and confession, deliverance will not occur despite our work. The temptation is to rush in and do something, but if nothing immediately happens we might give up or even pretend that all is well. The only remedy then is to repeat the work.

Dr. Frank Lake told me of an occasion when he met a severely depressed woman in a mental hospital. She had had an experience of the Holy Spirit at a local church, yet, after some months of real joy, she had plunged into depression. Her minister had concluded that she must be demon-possessed, and he immediately conducted a deliverance prayer. This had no effect, and so he repeated the exercise. The woman had a breakdown and ended up in the hospital.

After listening to her story, Dr. Lake felt that the Holy Spirit, in filling her life, also wanted to bring healing to the repressed hurts from her past. This made sense to her, so she shared her childhood hurts. She gained real healing and renewal. Far from a quick deliverance to bring her joy bouncing back, she needed someone who could listen before drawing conclusions. Deliverance is not a panacea for all ills, but a specific resource for a specific need.

How Long Does Deliverance Take?

How long, then, should the ministry last? Jesus' ministry seems to have had immediate effect, as did that of the disciples.

However, the disciples could not help the young boy mentioned in Mark 9, despite their collective prayer. They were puzzled, but Jesus told them, "This kind can come out only by prayer." Some manuscripts include the words "and fasting" (Mk 9:29, margin). The spirit possessing the boy was of a particularly strong kind, and prayer (and fasting) was needed as an extra preparation before ministry.

Most writers on deliverance mention that groups of spirits can bother people and that deliverance is won in stages (for example, as in Mt 12:45; Mk 5:9). Although this thought is not clearly developed in the Bible, we need to maintain an open mind on the subject and be prepared to discover if more than one spirit is at work.

Once, when I had seen a woman set free from a very strong spirit, I decided to offer a general prayer of cleansing. I asked that if there were any other spirits present in her life, they also would be bound and would leave her alone. I spoke calmly and assured the woman that she need not feel any pressure to repeat the earlier manifestations. More inner distress did surface and was quickly dealt with. A repetition of this prayer provoked no further reactions, and she felt at peace with herself and with the Lord.

As a rule, we should attempt to keep our actual prayers for deliverance as short as possible. If our prayers yield no manifestations, those being helped should be encouraged to consolidate their freedom and growth as Christians. It is important to maintain contact with them, especially if they belong to your church. If they belong to another church or fellowship, their own minister should be encouraged to follow up. Should other problems arise, those involved in the earlier ministry may be called together again in order to provide further help. This should be done only if the pastor thinks it necessary.

Epilog

Christians have the victory over evil through the triumph of Jesus Christ's death and resurrection. John writes that Jesus came to the earth in order to destroy the works of the devil (1 Jn 3:8). Paul, using the language of conquest, says that on the cross Jesus, "having disarmed the powers and authorities, . . . made a public spectacle of them, triumphing over them by the cross" (Col 3:15).

Because of what Jesus accomplished on the cross, and because he is the Lord of glory, his people can also be more than conquerors. When Jesus sent out the twelve on their first mission, he commanded them to cast out demons. When they returned from a similar mission some time later, it was their ability to cast out demons that caused their amazement at the power of Christ (Mt 10:1; Lk 10:17-20). The coming of the Holy Spirit in power on the church at Pentecost confirms that this ability is to be a continuing mission of the church and is not limited to the original mission of the early disciples.

Jesus, in the prayer he taught his disciples, cautioned them not to be led into temptation, and went on to add the petition, "But deliver us from evil" (Mt 6:13). This is a clear warning for believers to keep away from anything occultic. We must not fall into the trap of thinking that we should compete or debate with evil; we are called to destroy it!

People who have become aware that something is wrong in their emotional, mental or spiritual world have often traced the problem to an involvement with some form of the occult. Once this cause has been recognized, true freedom and healing have come in the name of Jesus. As Christians, we must know how to help and heal those who have been bound by the demonic world. In doing this, we follow in the footsteps of Jesus, of whom it is written: "God anointed Jesus of Nazareth with the Holy Spirit and power, and . . . he went around doing good and healing all who were under the power of the devil" (Acts 10:38).

Donald Bridge emphasizes that Christians are working between two victories: Calvary and the return of Jesus Christ. Our enemy is a defeated foe, thanks to the triumph of the cross and resurrection.[1] Our victory is like the Normandy landings in World War 2: it was the beginning of the end of the enemy's rule; it was only a matter of time before the war would be over. For us in Christ, the beachhead was established at Calvary when a massive deathblow was dealt to the enemy, and now we are engaged in the final skirmishes. The outcome is already determined and will be fully displayed when Christ returns for his own.

Our God reigns! We must focus on what Christ has done.

Jesus spoke of Satan falling like lightning as a result of the ministry of disciples powerfully anointed with the Holy Spirit. John says that Christians are "from God and have overcome them [the demonic world], because the one who is in you is greater than the one who is in the world" (1 Jn 4:4). Christ has triumphed over all, and he has called us to share in his amazing victory over evil. As Paul notes in 1 Corinthians 15:57:

Thanks be to God! He gives us the victory through our Lord Jesus Christ.

Notes

Chapter 1: The Occult Explosion

[1]*After Dark,* Channel 4, April 30, 1988.

[2]This is the British equivalent of the American Civil Liberties Union.

[3]The following passages clearly forbid the use of occult resources: Exodus 22:18 (the death penalty for sorcery, according to the Old Testament Law); Leviticus 19:31 (we are forbidden to consult mediums and spiritists); 20:6 (those who resort to the occult will be separated from God); Deuteronomy 18:9-12 (occult involvement makes us detestable to God); Isaiah 8:19-22 (occult involvement is ultimately unsatisfying and brings distress); 47:13-15 (occult power cannot save); Acts 15:16-18 (powers of fortunetelling are due to a demonic spirit); Galatians 5:20 (witchcraft is a sin that excludes us from the kingdom of God).

[4]Stuart Checkley, quoted in *Doorways to Danger* (Evangelical Alliance, 1987).

[5]David Porter, *Children at Risk* (Kingsway, 1986).

[6]"Devil Worship," *The Rossendale Free Press,* October 4, 1986.

[7]*Focus,* Central Television, 1988.

Chapter 2: Know Your Enemy

[1]Frank and Ida Mae Hammond, *Pigs in the Parlour* (Impact Books, 1973), pp. 113-15.

[2]William P. Wilson, "Hysteria and Demons," in John Warwick Montgomery, ed., *Demon Possession* (Bethany House Publishers, 1976), pp. 223-31.

[3]M. Scott Peck, *People of the Lie* (Simon & Schuster, 1985), pp. 39-40.

Chapter 3: Occult Doors I: Superstition and Fortunetelling

[1]John Richards, *But Deliver Us from Evil* (Darton, Longman and Todd, 1974), p. 46.

[2]Kurt Koch, *Between Christ and Satan* (Kregel Publications, 1969).

[3]Obtainable from ACT, 21 Romeland Hill, St. Albans, Hertfordshire, AL3 4ET, England.

[4]Richards, *But Deliver Us from Evil*, p. 47.

[5]Genesis 11:1-4. Other passages which condemn stargazing are Leviticus 19:31; Deuteronomy 4:19; Isaiah 47:13-15; Acts 7:43.

[6]Ronald Reagan, along with other Hollywood entertainers such as Marlene Dietrich, Tyrone Power and Peter Lawford, was known to be influenced by the astrological writings of Carroll Righter in the 1940s.

[7]Kurt Koch, *Christian Counselling and Occultism* (Evangelization Publishers, 1972), p. 163.

Chapter 4: Occult Doors II: Spiritism and Magic

[1]Quoted in Ralph Gasson, *The Challenging Counterfeit* (Logos International, 1966), p. 23.

[2]Ibid., p. 22.

[3]Ibid., p. 26.

[4]Bishop Pike, *The Other Side* (W. H. Allen, 1969).

[5]Kurt Koch, *Occult Bondage and Deliverance,* quoted in John Richards, *But Deliver Us from Evil* (Darton, Longman and Todd, 1974), p. 73.

[6]Ralph Gasson relates how, as a former medium, he was blinded for nearly twenty-four hours after such an encounter. In Gasson, *The Challenging Counterfeit,* p. 74.

[7]Hugh Trowell, *Diseases of Strain and Stress,* quoted in Richards, *But Deliver Us from Evil,* pp. 85-86.

[8]Doreen Irvine, *Spiritual Warfare* (Marshall Pickering, 1986), pp. 92-104.

[9]*Friday Night Live,* Central Television, 13 May 1988.

[10]For a fuller and clearer treatment of this complex issue, see the leaflet *Witchcraft and Satanism,* obtainable from CRO, PO Box 150, Bromley, Kent, UK.

[11]Doreen Irvine, *From Witchcraft to Christ* (Concordia, 1973).

[12]Quoted in Richards, *But Deliver Us from Evil,* p. 78.

[13]Martyn Lloyd-Jones, *The Christian Warfare* (Banner of Truth, 1982), p. 6.

Chapter 5: The Occult Attraction

[1]Doreen Irvine, *From Witchcraft to Christ* (Concordia, 1973).

[2]*Missionary Herald,* February 1985, p. 29.

[3]Billy Graham, *The Jesus Generation* (Hodder and Stoughton, 1972).

[4]Richard Foster, *Money, Sex and Power* (Hodder and Stoughton, 1986), p. 176.

[5]John Richards, *But Deliver Us from Evil* (Darton, Longman and Todd, 1974), p. 62.

[6]Ralph Gasson, *The Challenging Counterfeit* (Logos International, 1966), p. 45.

Chapter 6: Why the Occult Works

[1]Michael Perry, ed., *Deliverance* (SPCK, 1987), pp. 44-45.

[2]See chapter one, note 8.

[3]Ephesians 2:2 (KJV); Acts 26:17-18; 2 Corinthians 4:4; Hebrews 2:14-15.

[4]See also Jude 6; 2 Peter 2:4.

[5]Mark 5:9, 12; James 2:19.

[6]Luke 11:24 speaks of them deciding to return to a place they had formerly occupied.

[7]For a fuller explanation, read Ralph Gasson, *The Challenging Counterfeit* (Logos International, 1966).

Chapter 7: Signals of Distress: Discernment before Ministry

[1]Kurt Koch, *Demonology Past and Present* (Kregel Publications, 1973), p. 85.

[2]William P. Wilson, "Hysteria and Demons," in John Warwick Montgomery, ed., *Demon Possession* (Bethany House Publishers, 1976), pp. 230ff.

[3]Some helpful guidelines to distinguishing between demonic activity and mental illness can be found in John Richards, *But Deliver Us from Evil* (Darton, Longman and Todd, 1974), p. 158.

[4]Matthew 4:24; Luke 6:18-19; 7:21.

[5]Michael Harper, *Spiritual Warfare* (Hodder and Stoughton, 1976), p. 96.

[6]*The Alternative Service Book* (SPCK, 1980), p. 230.

Chapter 8: Preparing for Ministry

[1]See John Richards, *But Deliver Us from Evil* (Darton, Longman and Todd, 1974), pp. 91f. Graham Twelftree provides a fuller definition in *Christ Triumphant* (Hodder and Stoughton, 1985), pp. 177-78, 215.

[2]Richards, *But Deliver Us from Evil,* p. 121.

[3]See also Ephesians 6:12-13.

[4]Michael Ross-Watson, "Can a Christian Be Demon-Possessed?" (unpublished paper).

[5]Michael Harper, *Spiritual Warfare* (Hodder and Stoughton, 1976), p. 109.

[6]Luke 22:3-4; John 13:26-27.

[7]The phenomenon of the effects of a curse put on a family member surviving down the family line are well documented. Deuteronomy 27—28 describes blessings and cursings which God pledged to send according to whether his covenant was kept or not. This is a sobering thought; the curse includes sickness and disease, mental breakdown and the breaking up of families.

Before we accuse God of vindictiveness, we should see these chapters in the light of Galatians 6:7-8: "Do not be deceived: God cannot be mocked. A man reaps what he sows. The one who sows to please his sinful nature, from that nature will reap destruction; the one who sows to please the Spirit, from the Spirit will reap eternal life."

[8]Harper, *Spiritual Warfare,* pp. 11-12.

[9]This raises the question whether Christians can be bothered by evil spirits in this way. The following references indicate that this is indeed possible: 2 Corinthians 11:3-4; 1 Timothy 4:1; Acts 5:3; Ephesians 4:27; James 3:14-16.

Chapter 9: Christian Deliverance Ministry

[1]Charles Sherlock, *The Overcoming of Satan* (Grove Books, 1986).

[2]Matthew 28:18-20; Luke 9:1-6; 10:1-12, 17-20.

Chapter 10: Praying for Deliverance

[1]Michael Green, *I Believe in Satan's Downfall* (Hodder and Stoughton, 1981), p. 139.

[2]Leon Suenens, *Renewal and the Powers of Darkness* (Darton, Longman and Todd, 1983), p. 17.

[3]Basilea Schlink, *Repentance: The Joy-filled Life* (Oliphants, 1969), pp. 20-21.

[4]Derek Prince, quoted in Frank and Ida Mae Hammond, *Pigs in the Parlour* (Impact Books, 1973), p. 107.

[5]Taken from "A Rite of Deliverance," South Africa.

[6]Hebrews 2:14-15. See also Colossians 2:15, which also considers the victory of the cross.

[7]Donald Bridge, *Power Evangelism and the Word of God* (Kingsway, 1987),

p. 183. See also 2 Corinthians 4:4.

[8]John Wimber, *Power Evangelism* (Hodder and Stoughton, 1985).

Chapter 11: Signs of Deliverance

[1]Mark 1:23-24; see also Luke 4:33-34.

[2]Mark 3:11; see also 5:6; 9:18, 20.

[3]Graham and Shirley Powell, *Christian, Set Yourself Free* (Center Mountain Ministries, 1983), p. 124.

[4]For example, Matthew 4:24; 9:32; Mark 6:13; Luke 13:10-13; Acts 16:18.

Epilog

[1]Donald Bridge, *Power Evangelism and the Word of God* (Kingsway, 1987), p. 198.

Bibliography

Bridge, Donald. *Power Evangelism and the Word of God.* Kingsway, 1987.

Forrest, Alistair and Peter Sanderson. *Cults and the Occult Today.* Marshall, Morgan and Scott, 1982.

Gasson, Ralph. *The Challenging Counterfeit.* Logos International, 1968.

Green, Michael. *I Believe in Satan's Downfall.* Hodder and Stoughton, 1981.

Harper, Michael. *Spiritual Warfare.* Hodder and Stoughton, 1970.

Koch, Kurt. *Demonology Past and Present.* Kregel Publications, 1973.

Montgomery, John Warwick, ed. *Demon Possession.* Bethany House Publishers, 1976.

Perry, Michael, ed. *Deliverance.* SPCK, 1987.

Powell, Graham and Shirley. *Christian, Set Yourself Free.* Center Mountain Ministries, 1983.

Richards, John. *But Deliver Us from Evil.* Darton, Longman and Todd, 1974.

Sherlock, Charles. *The Overcoming of Satan.* Grove Books, 1986.

Twelftree, Graham. *Christ Triumphant.* Hodder and Stoughton, 1985.